TO STUDY AND TO TEACH

The Methodology of
Nechama Leibowitz

To Study and to Teach

The Methodology of
Nechama Leibowitz

SHMUEL PEERLESS

THE LOOKSTEIN CENTER, SCHOOL OF EDUCATION, BAR-ILAN UNIVERSITY
מרכז לוקשטיין, בית ספר לחינוך, אוניברסיטת בר-אילן

URIM PUBLICATIONS
Jerusalem • New York

To Study and to Teach: The Methodology of Nechama Leibowitz
By Shmuel Peerless

ISBN 965-7108-55-1

The Lookstein Center, School of Education, Bar Ilan University
Ramat Gan 52900 Israel
www.Lookstein.org

Lambda Publishers, Inc.
3709 13th Avenue, Brooklyn, New York 11218 USA
Tel: 718-972-5449 Fax: 718-972-6307 mh@ejudaica.com

Urim Publications, P.O. Box 52287, Jerusalem 91521 Israel

www.UrimPublications.com

CONTENTS

We deeply appreciate the patronage of
The Estate of
Belia Reutlinger
and the
American Friends of Bar Ilan University
for their support of this project.

FOREWORD

As a result of the publication of her *Studies in Parshat Hashavua*, Nechama Leibowitz has become widely recognized as one of the most influential Torah scholars of the 20th century. Yet, her influence on Torah scholarship in our generation is even greater than it appears. For approximately thirty years, Nechama published study sheets (*gilyonot*) on the weekly Torah portion which she distributed to students throughout the world. In the *gilyonot*, Nechama presented selections from the text and from the commentaries with probing questions designed to guide the readers through a textual analysis that would deepen their understanding of the passage. Over the years, literally thousands of individuals would submit answers to Nechama's *gilyonot* by mail, and Nechama would correct and return them. Many of these students were teachers of Torah in both Israel and the Diaspora who had studied with Nechama in her university courses or seminars for teachers.

Nechama was the teachers' teacher, and her insights on methodology have been utilized by educators throughout the world. Nevertheless, Nechama's unique approach to Torah instruction has never been comprehensively and systematically presented in one work. This volume attempts to fill that void by organizing Nechama's methodological teachings and pedagogical techniques in a manner that makes them easily accessible. The information provided in this work is collected and extrapolated from Nechama's lectures, published writings, and *gilyonot*. Most of the examples given are from Nechama's own writings. A small number were derived by the author through the application of Nechama's methodology. A complete list of sources is provided at the end of the book.

It is hoped, that in addition to presenting Nechama's pedagogical methodology, some of the personal qualities of this master teacher and Torah scholar will be evident between the lines. As such, Nechama the teacher, scholar, and person will be preserved as an inspiration to future generations of Torah teachers.

Note: In a number of instances, variations among the commentators are based on grammatical nuances within the text. It is, therefore, difficult in some of these cases to provide a translation of the verse, as the translation itself represents an interpretation. In such situations, we have included a specific translation with an indication of its source as an indication that it is actually one of a number of possible translations. The original Hebrew text is provided in these cases to enable the reader to easily refer to the original source.

Answers provided to the questions throughout this work are suggested answers formulated by the author or by others of Nechama's students. Although they are often based on Nechama's teachings, they were not written by her.

Acknowledgements

I would like to take this opportunity to acknowledge a number of people who have contributed significantly to this work. I express my deepest appreciation to Professors Gavriel H. Cohen and Ruth Ben Meir for their ongoing review of this manuscript, and for their suggestions and comments which have helped to give direction to this project and ensure its accuracy. A special thanks to Yitshak Reiner for his contribution of suggested answers to Nechama's questions in chapter four of this work, as well as his ongoing help and partnership in enhancing my understanding of Nechama's methodology. A special thanks as well to Rabbi Scot Berman, whose review of this work and suggestions helped to give direction to this project, and ensure its relevance to teachers in the field. Similarly, I express my appreciation to Rabbi Jay Goldmintz and Mrs. Barbara Freedman for reviewing the manuscript and providing their insights.

I would also like to take this opportunity to thank Rabbi Stuart Zweiter and my other colleagues at the Lookstein Center for their support of the completion and publication of this work. Special thanks as well to the American Friends of Bar Ilan for their generous support of this publication.

Last, but certainly not least, I wish to express my love and appreciation to my wife, Jo Ann, and to my daughters, Shoshana, Alta, Sara, and Yehudit, who not only have provided me continuously with love, support and inspiration, but have also, as my best chavrutot, contributed significantly to the development of my Torah learning.

CHAPTER I

NECHAMA LEIBOWITZ'S METHODOLOGY: AN OVERVIEW

Introduction

It is not by chance that an observer of a *shiur* (class) given by Nechama Liebowitz would have found all of the participants actively involved in the learning. For one thing, Nechama required everyone present to record his/her answers to the questions that she posed. She would personally check many of the answers and give immediate oral or written feedback. But, in reality, the involvement in Nechama's classes related more to other aspects of her teaching methodology. Nechama believed that true learning takes place only when students are engaged in a thought provoking process of analysis. She opposed the rote learning that is manifested in much of the instructional material on the teaching of Torah. It was Nechama's selection of texts and commentaries, her presentation of the material, and the types of questions that she asked which most engaged her students. Thus, Nechama's students, many themselves teachers of Torah, absorbed not only the content of her lessons, but her unique methodology as well. This work is dedicated to the presentation and preservation of that methodology.

The Goals of Torah Instruction

Nechama identified four goals of Torah learning in ascending order:

1. the accumulation of factual knowledge
2. the development of independent learning skills
3. the development of a love of Torah learning
4. the observance of *mitzvot*

The third goal was in Nechama's mind primary with regard to Torah instruction. She stressed that although the observance of the *mitzvot* is the most important goal of Torah learning, the teacher of Torah is limited in this area. Rather, success in instilling a love of Torah learning will in itself lead to the fulfillment of *mitzvot*. The accomplishment of all of the goals is dependent on the pedagogical methods employed by the teacher.

Active Learning

Nechama believed that in order to fulfill these goals, the teacher must involve the student in active learning. In active learning, the teacher serves as a facilitator of learning rather than as a repository and transmitter of knowledge. Nechama posited that activities which are designed to have students absorb information from an external source ultimately have a minimal impact on learning. But, how does one engage students actively in the study of Torah? While active learning is easy to achieve in the science laboratory, it is much more difficult to create in a Torah lesson. Nechama suggested several "trickim" (as she called them), strategies designed to achieve that goal. This work presents a number of her pedagogical tips.

"The Prohibitions"

Accordingly, Nechama listed five common practices from which teachers should refrain:

1. Do not lecture: The lecture format is the classical model of frontal teaching in which the teacher transmits information to the students. In Nechama's opinion, very little learning takes place using that format. Rather, students must be actively involved in alternative learning activities.

2. Do not allow students to write while you are speaking: The fact that students are writing does not indicate that they are learning. On the contrary, taking notes while the teacher is talking can in fact prevent analytical thinking and learning from taking place. If the student has effectively absorbed the information discussed, he/she will be able to transcribe it afterwards if necessary.

3. Do not give an introduction to the material that is to be studied: Teachers often introduce a unit by providing background information and/or summarizing the material to be studied. Nechama opposed introductions of this nature not only because they are frontal, but also because they may reduce opportunities for discovery. When it is valuable for students to get an overview of the entire section before delving into particulars, she favored the use of alternative activities that would force the students to independently preview the section. A number of these introductory methods are presented in chapter 2.

4. Do not ask students to answer factual questions or to paraphrase: Nechama believed that it is not worthwhile to ask any question where the answer is obvious from the context. Rather, questions should be thought provoking, requiring the student to demonstrate an understanding of the material. For example, on the verse that states: "And Yaacov went out of Beer Sheva and he went toward Haran" (Bereishit 28:10), Nechama would consider it ineffective to ask students questions like "From where did Yaacov leave?" or "To where did Yaacov travel?" These are questions that the students could answer correctly without really understanding what has happened in the story. Rather, one might give students a map and asked them if Yaacov traveled east or west? Or, students might be asked to compare this verse to Bereshit 12:4-5 in which Avraham travels from Haran to Canaan. By tracing the routes of Avraham and Yaacov on the map, the students would see that they have taken opposite routes. This comparison raises the possibility of other thought provoking questions that are appropriate even for young students. The types of questions that Nechama advocated are presented systematically in chapter 4. Other examples can be found throughout this work.

5.   Do not use a repetitive lesson structure: Nechama believed that even effective learning activities and questions should not be used in a repetitive fashion. A repetitive style tends to generate routine learning patterns, reducing active involvement on the part of the student. For this reason, Nechama was critical of most Chumash workbooks, which tend to be repetitive and do not place the student in a position of responsibility for learning. The teacher must draw on a repertoire of effective questions and learning activities as they are appropriate to the particular text being studied.

Selecting Texts

Nechama taught that lessons should be varied both in terms of content and style. As such, she advocated a relatively rapid pace in covering Biblical texts. This in itself presents a challenge to the teacher. One could spend weeks, or even months, studying particular sections. Nechama, however, warned against spending too much time on a specific section, particularly in the elementary or high school setting. In an article on the teaching of "Akeidat Yitzchak," Nechama indicated that it might be studied for several weeks with adults, but should be covered in the course of a few days with younger students. This requires the teacher to select a particular focus in terms of topics covered and supplementary texts and commentaries utilized.

> "The teacher has to decide what to leave out and what topics should not be touched, because it is pointless to tackle a number of different topics and problems superficially or incidentally in a chapter. It is preferable to concentrate on just a few topics, but in depth."[1]

The types of texts, *Midrashim*, and commentaries that Nechama selected for instruction generally fall into several categories:

1. Texts that allow for comparison with other Biblical sections: These texts provide the opportunity for students to engage in an internal textual analysis. Nechama's methodology of textual comparison is discussed in depth in chapter 5.

2. Sections which contain textual difficulties (קושיות): Textual difficulty is the starting point for much of Biblical commentary. In chapter 6, we examine several such קושיות in depth. A list of common textual difficulties is included in Appendix 3.

3. Sections which exhibit unique Biblical literary style: The literary style of the Torah reflects unique formats that can contain additional layers of meaning. Several of these stylistic features are examined in chapter 7.

4. *Midrashim* and commentaries that help to better understand the text: Nechama's approach to selecting appropriate exegeti-

---

[1] *Torah Insights*, Eliner Library, Jerusalem, 1995, p. 22

cal material for instruction is touched upon in chapters 3 and 4.

5. Texts that contain a significant educational message: This criterion was of primary importance to Nechama. She believed that lessons must be built around educational messages that resonate with the students and find application and relevance in their lives.

Two model lessons are presented in chapters 8 and 9 in order to demonstrate the implementation of Nechama's methodology in lesson preparation. Chapter 8 deals with a legal section, Vayikra 19:1–18, and chapter 9 deals with a narrative section, chapter 4 of Bereishit.

CHAPTER II

INTRODUCING THE UNIT

The purpose of the introductory lesson is to provide the context, to give an overview of the chapter or section to be studied before examining the details. In place of the teacher providing the students with background information, Nechama suggested that students be given an assignment that would require them to independently read and think about the section being studied. The following are a few examples:

1. Tell the students to imagine that they are putting on a play about this section, and to consider one of the following questions:

a. How many set changes would you need in this play?

b. Who is the most important character in the play?

c. What tone of voice would character X employ in his/her part?

Example: Chapter 34 in Bereishit relating to the abduction of Dinah provides a good opportunity for the use of these methodologies.

a. The chapter includes five changes of set – 1) the field, 2) the house of Shechem, 3) the house of Yaacov, 4) the city of Shechem, and 5) the house of Yaacov.

b. It might be a challenge for students to decide who is the main character of the story. Is it Yaacov who struggles with the conflict between his daughter's welfare and his family's relations with the local population, is it Dina whose safety is at stake, or is it Shimon and Levi who defend their sister's honor?

c. If asked to determine Yaacov's tone of voice, students would have to consider his reaction to different aspects of the story – the tone of his response to the news, of his discussion with Chamor, and his discussion with Shimon and Levi following the massacre.

These three exercises become progressively more sophisticated. The first exercise requires students to review the facts of the story. The second exercise requires some literary analysis and judgement. The third exercise requires psychological analysis.

2. Ask the students to provide a title for the section being studied.

Example: Chapter 34 in Bereishit also provides a good example for the employment of this technique. There are numerous possibilities for titles including: 1) "The Abduction of Dinah", 2) "Yaacov's Dilemma", 3) "Shimon and Levi to the Rescue", etc. This exercise requires the students to give an opinion regarding the focus of the section.

3. Ask the students to identify the key verse in the section.

Example: A unit on the sixth day of creation, Bereishit 1:24–31, might be introduced with this type of exercise. In this case, it is probable that students will focus on one of two issues: 1) the creation of man, or 2) the completion of the creation process. If the student focuses on the creation of man, he/she might select verse 27 which emphasizes the fact that man was created in the image of God, verse 28 which focuses on man's relationship with the rest of creation, or verse 26 which introduces the collaborative nature of the creation of man. The student who focuses on the completion of creation might select verse 31, which demonstrates God's great satisfaction with his creation.

4. Have the students divide the section into different parts. In some cases, the teacher might want to request a certain number of divisions, or may propose a specific division and ask the students to justify or oppose it.

Examples: The following are two examples of the use of this methodology:

a. Shemot: Chapter 1

8) Now there arose over Egypt a new king who knew not Yosef.

9) And he said to his people: "Behold, the people of the Children of Israel are more and mightier than we.

10) Come, let us deal wisely with them, lest they multiply and it come to pass that, when any war should chance, they also join our enemies and fight against us and go up from the land."

11) Therefore, they did set over them taskmasters to afflict them with their burdens, and they built for Paroah treasure cities, Pitom and Ramses.

12) But the more they afflicted them, the more they multiplied and grew and they were mortified on account of the Children of Israel.

13) And the Egyptians made the Children of Israel work with rigor.

14) And they embittered their lives with hard bondage, in mortar, and   brick, and all manner of bondage in the field; all their bondage wherein they made them work was with rigor.

15) And the king of Egypt spoke to the Hebrew midwives, of whom the name of one was Shifra and the name of the other was Puah;

16) And he said: "When you deliver the Hebrew women and you look at the birthstones, if it be a son you shall kill him, and if it is a daughter you shall let her live."

17) But the midwives feared God, and did not as the king of Egypt had commanded them, but saved the male children alive.

18) And the king of Egypt called the midwives and said to them: "Why have you done this thing and saved the male children alive?"

19) And the midwives said to Paroah: "Because the Hebrew women are not as the Egyptian women; for they are lively and are delivered before the midwives come to them."

20) Therefore, God dealt well with the midwives, and the people multiplied and grew very mighty.

21) And it came to pass, because the midwives feared God, that he made them houses.

22) And Paroah charged all of his people saying, "Every son that is born you shall cast into the river, and every daughter you shall save alive."

Shemot 1:8–22 recounts the beginning of the enslavement of Bnai Yisrael in Egypt. If students are asked to divide this section into its component parts, they must begin to identify and analyze the various stages of the oppression of the Jews. For example, should the first division be verses 8–10 or 8–14? This question hinges on whether Pharoah's discussion with the people is an independent stage of the process. Similarly, should verses 15–22 be viewed as one section, or should verse 22 be viewed independently? That is to say, do Pharoah's actions in verse 22 reflect an initiative that is significantly different than his attempted manipulation of the midwives? Obviously, further subdivision of these sections must be considered as well. This activity helps the students to better understand the text and prepares them for questions raised by Rashi and Ramban on this section.

b. This method can be used as well in studying halachic sections of the Torah as, for example, in studying the Ten Commandments. Prior to beginning the inodepth study, students could be asked to divide the commandments into two categories, and then into three categories. The following are some of the possibilities that the students might generate:

Two categories:

Example A. 1. positive commandments
2. negative commandments

Example B. 1. *mitzvot* between man and God
2. *mitzvot* between man & man

Three categories:

Example A. 1. *mitzvot* that relate to speech
2. *mitzvot* that relate to thought
3. *mitzvot* that relate to action

Example B. 1. *mitzvot* relating to the holiness of God
2. *mitzvot* relating to the holiness of man
3. *mitzvot* relating to the holiness of time

This activity also alludes to a number of questions raised by the commentators, such as: Is "I am the Lord your God" actually a commandment? Is it possible to command something that is only fulfilled in thought? Are honoring your parents and observing shabbat considered to be between man & man or between man & God? Is shabbat a positive or a negative commandment?

Obviously, the selection of an activity for the introductory lesson must be age appropriate and appropriate to the nature of the text being studied. It is helpful, as well, if the activity is consistent with the commentaries that the teacher plans to introduce. Once the students have completed the introductory activity, they should be asked to explain and justify their answers.

This type of exercise accomplishes several things:

1. It requires the student to study the entire section and to give thought to the content.

2. It validates the ability of the learner to generate ideas. The focus is not on which answers are right or wrong, but how well they can be justified.

3. It raises issues of interest, many of which may be dealt with by the commentators.

Having acquired an overview of the section, the students are now prepared to study the text in greater detail. The chapters that follow present a number of Nechama's methodological approaches to effective text study.

CHAPTER III

THE ROLE OF MIDRASH IN TORAH INSTRUCTION

Introduction

There has been an ongoing debate among Torah educators regarding the role of Midrash in Torah instruction. Many have expressed the concern that the mixing of Biblical and Rabbinic texts confuses the students who are at times unable to distinguish between what actually appears in the text and what is Rabbinic extrapolation. Nechama was not concerned with this issue. Her response to those who raised the question was "אז מה?!" – "So what?" So what if the student learns Midrash and is unable to make the distinction? At least he/she has learned something valuable, and he/she will be able to make the distinction at a later stage.

Midrash as Parshanut

Nechama was a pioneer in recognizing and presenting Rabbinic literature as an expression of Biblical exegesis on the same level as the medieval commentators.[1] In her written works, Nechama draws on over 700 *Midrashim*, over 300 citations from the Gemara, and over 1,000 Rabbinic dictums. This approach to Midrash was certainly not popular among Biblical scholars and teachers of parshanut of her time, who viewed Midrash largely as homiletical in

---

[1] For a full discussion of this topic, see:
"הפרשנות המדרשית במפעלה התורני של נחמה לייבוביץ" by Gavriel H. Cohen, in **פרקי נחמה**, Eliner Press, World Zionist Organization, 2001, pp. 93–108.

nature with little relationship to the simple meaning of the text. Nechama also valued Midrash for its ability to express the more emotional side of the Biblical narrative and to translate Biblical philosophy and values into a context more relevant to the reader.

Nevertheless, Nechama did not advocate the teaching of just any Midrash in a haphazard fashion. Rather, she advocates the use of *Midrashim* that are grounded in the Biblical text and that deepen our understanding of the verse. She indicates that *Midrashim* which destroy the Biblical sentence structure or which are disconnected from the verses preceding and following the sentence should not be taught, even if they teach a very nice message. It is, therefore, important for teachers to be discerning in their selection of *Midrashim* for instruction, and to help direct the students to the exegetical value of the *Midrashim* that are taught.

The Use of *Midrashim* by the Classical Commentators

Similarly, Nechama felt it worthwhile to try to foster an understanding of the use of *Midrashim* by the classical commentators who viewed themselves as proponents of פשוטו של מקרא, explaining the simple meaning of the text.

This issue is critical in studying the commentary of Rashi, one of the leading proponents of the school of פשוטו של מקרא, who made extensive use of *Midrashim* in his commentary. Rashi's commentary is clearly the focal point of most Chumash curricula. Yet, many find it difficult to understand and adequately transmit the innovation that Rashi introduced to Torah study. Seventy percent of Rashi's commentary is drawn from Rabbinic literature, and, as such, one might question whether he really reflects the approach of "פשוטו של מקרא". On the other hand, Rashi frequently refrains from using Midrashim even when they are available. In order to foster a more sophisticated understanding of

"פשט" as it manifests itself in Rashi's commentary, it is necessary to understand his selective use of Midrash.

Rashi's Use of Midrash – Homiletics or Interpretation?[2]

The super-commentaries on Rashi differ regarding the role of Midrash in Rashi's commentary. Some contend that Rashi refers to *Midrashim* both to explain a difficulty in the text, but also to teach a lesson. In other words, some of the *Midrashim* brought by Rashi are necessary to properly understand the text, while others are supplemental embellishments to the text. Other commentators, on the contrary, claim that Rashi only quotes *Midrashim* when they are necessary to understand difficulties in the text.

Nechama clearly subscribes to the second position. She claims that Rashi is systematic in his use of Midrash. Rashi, however did not write an explanatory introduction to his commentary, and it thus falls on the reader to understand his approach through an analysis of the commentary. Nechama believes that the key to understanding Rashi's system is to pay attention to those situations in which Rashi rejects the use of existent *Midrashim* and those instances in which he selects one Midrash over another. The methodological implications are clear. By guiding the student through such an analysis, the teacher will simultaneously engage the student in a meaningful learning process.

Rashi's Criteria for the Use of *Midrashim*

Nechama posits that for Rashi to utilize a particular Midrash in his commentary, it has to meet two criteria:

---

[2] This topic is discussed by Nechama in an article entitled: "דרכו של רש״י בהבאת מדרשים בפירושו לתורה" which appears in *Lilmod Ulelamed Tanakh*, Eliner Press, WZO, Jerusalem, 1996.

1. It must answer a particular difficulty in the text (i.e., a grammatical inconsistency, a redundancy, a divergence from the context, a theological difficulty, a divergence from the chronology, etc.).

2. It must fit in to the context of the larger section within which the verse appears.

In this sense, Rashi the *pashtan* differs from the *darshanim* who preceded him. The *darshanim* explained verses in order to teach a particular lesson, similar to rabbinic sermons today. As such, the *drasha* can utilize a verse out of context and does not have to be consistent with other *drashot*. Rashi's innovation is that he explains the verse as part of a larger whole, selecting only *Midrashim* that when pieced together create a unified picture. Thus, while Rashi's commentary may appear at times to be simplistic, it is, in Nechama's opinion, a sophisticated work of scholarship. The tapestry of grammatical, literary, and Midrashic explanations that Rashi presents is, in his opinion, the simple meaning of the text.

Explicit Evidence –
Instances in Which Rashi Rejects Existent *Midrashim*

When Rashi utilizes the term "פשוטו כמשמעו" (the simple meaning is the same as the literal meaning) he is implying that in this instance, the literal meaning is to be favored over a Midrashic explanation. The implication is clear – in other instances the Midrashic explanation, and not the literal translation, is indeed the simple meaning of the text. Thus, Rashi's statement of "פשוטו כמשמעו" is an invitation to analyze the existing *Midrashim* to understand why Rashi did not see them as suitable for inclusion in his commentary. Nechama points out several places in which Rashi discusses explicitly his rejection of specific *Midrashim*, such as Bereishit 3:8, Bereishit 4:8, Bereishit 49:22 and Shemot 23:2. As an example, let us

examine the way in which Nechama would suggest teaching Bereishit 4:8 in order to give students a greater appreciation of Rashi's
methodology:

> "ויאמר קין אל הבל אחיו ויהי בהיותם בשדה ויקם קין אל הבל
> אחיו ויהרגהו".

"And Cain said to Hevel his brother, and it came to pass
when they were in the field and Cain rose up against Hevel
his brother and slew him."

> **רש"י:** נכנס עמו בדברי ריב ומצה להתעולל עליו ולהרגו. ויש
> בזה מדרש אגדה, אך זה יישובו של המקרא.

Rashi: He started to argue and fight with him in order to
fall on him and kill him. There is Midrash on this, but the
above is the plain meaning of the verse.

Students should be asked to identify the difficulty in the text that
Rashi is addressing. Clearly, some important information is seemingly missing from the text. The Torah refers to a conversation that
took place between Cain and Hevel, but then fails to record the
content of the conversation. The students should now be presented with the Midrash that Rashi does not utilize and analyze
why he rejects it. The following Midrash from Midrash Rabbah
records three possible conversations that might have taken place
between Cain and Hevel:

> ויאמר קין אל הבל אחיו ויהי בהיותם בשדה - על מה היו
> מדיינים? אמרו: בואו ונחלוק את העולם. אחד נטל את
> הקרקעות ואחד נטל את המיטלטלין. דין אמר: ארעא דאת
> קאם עלה-דידי (זה אמר: הארץ אשר אתה עומד עליה שלי
> היא). ודין אמר: מה דאת לבש- דידי (וזה אמר: מה שאתה לובש
> שלי הוא). דין אמר: חלוץ! דין אמר: פרח! מתוך כך: "ויקם קין
> אל הבל אחיו ויהרגהו".

ר׳ יהושע דסכנין בשם ר׳ לוי אמר: שניהם נטלו את
הקרקעות, ושניהם נטלו את המיטלטלין. ועל מה היו מידיינין?
אלא זה אומר: בתחומי בית המקדש ייבנה, וזה אומר: בתחומי
בית המקדש ייבנה...ומתוך כך "ויקם קין אל הבל אחיו
ויהרגהו".
יהודה בר׳ אמי אמר: על חוה הראשונה היו מידיינין.

Then Cain said to Hevel while they were in the field. What
were they arguing about? They said: Come and let us divide
up the world. One took the land and the other took the
movable property. The former said: 'The land that you are
standing on belongs to me', and the latter said: 'The clothes
that you are wearing belong to me'. The latter said: 'Take
them off !', and the former said: 'Get off !'. The result:
'Cain rose up against his brother Hevel and killed him.'

Rabbi Yehoshua of Sakhnin quotes R. Levi: Each took
both land and movable property. What did they argue
about? One said: 'The Temple will be built on my property', and the other said: 'The Temple will be built on my
property'.... As a result, 'Cain rose up against Hevel his
brother and killed him.

Yehudah the son of R. Ami: They were arguing over
Chava....

Students should be asked to analyze the differences between the
three arguments described in the Midrash. Each Midrash identifies
a different source of the conflict between Cain and Hevel. According to the first opinion it is the ownership of property, according to
the second it is the desire for religious supremacy, and according to
the third it is the desire for a woman. This Midrash posits that
competition over wealth, religion, and sex are the primary sources
of conflict in the world.

While Rashi may agree with this homiletic message, he cannot
consider any of the opinions to be the simple meaning of the text.

The students should be asked why these opinions are unacceptable to Rashi. All three of the cases adequately solve the difficulty in the text by providing the missing conversation. None of them, however, are consistent with the larger context. In the Midrashic accounts, both protagonists are equally responsible for the argument. In the Torah account, however, Cain is clearly the antagonist and bears responsibility for precipitating the argument. This is suggested, as well, by the fact that the verse begins with the phrase "And Cain said to Hevel". It is for this reason that Rashi rejects the Midrash. Rashi does not suggest an alternative conversation since the content of the argument is not significant. Cain simply precipitated an argument as a pretext to attack his brother.

Implicit Evidence – Selective Use of Midrash

There are many instances in which Rashi makes selective use of *Midrashim* without explicitly referring to the process. In some cases, a Midrash refers to several verses in the Torah but is only quoted by Rashi in reference to one or some of the verses. In other cases, Rashi may transfer a Midrash from the verse for which it was originally addressed to another verse. And, of course, many times Rashi refrains from utilizing available *Midrashim* without referring to them. Through an analysis of these instances, students can gain further insight into Rashi's concept of "פשוטו של מקרא".

Let us examine a prototypical case. The Midrash often identifies anonymous people in the Torah with well known personalities. For example, the refugee who brings a report to Avraham is identified as Og the King of Bashan (Bereishit 14:13), the two lads who accompany Avraham and Yitzchak to the Akeidah are identified as Yishmael and Eliezer (Bereishit 22:3), and the wood gatherer who violates shabbat is identified as Tzlafchad (Bamidbar 15:32). In some cases, Rashi utilizes the Midrashic identification and in some

cases he does not. Let us look at one such section and how it might
be taught:

"וישארו שני אנשים במחנה שם האחד אלדד ושם השני מידד
ותנח עלהם הרוח והמה בכתובים ולא יצאו האהלה ויתנבאו
במחנה. וירץ הנער ויגד למשה ויאמר אלדד ומידד מתנבאים
במחנה ויען יהושע בן נון משרת משה מבחריו ויאמר אדני, משה
כלאם"."

"And there remained two men in the camp, the name of
one was Eldad and the name of the other was Medad. And
the spirit rested on them... and the prophesized in the
camp. And the young man ran ("וירץ הנער") and told
Moshe and said: 'Eldad and Medad are prophesizing in the
camp. And Yehoshua Bin Nun, the servant of Moshe from
his youth answered and said: 'My master Moshe restrain
them.'" (Bamidbar 11:26–28)

Rashi identifies the lad who reports to Moshe as his son Gershom.
This is consistent with one opinion brought by the Midrash. The
Sifre identifies the lad as Yehoshua based on the fact that he is
referred to as "נער" elsewhere (Shemot 33:11). The Tanchuma
identifies the lad as Gershom. The students should be asked to
analyze why Rashi chose to identify the lad as Gershom rather than
Yehoshua, and why he felt the need to identify the lad at all. The
first question can be answered by looking at the continuation of
the text: "And Yehoshua answered...." Certainly Yehoshua would
not answer himself. Thus, the context forces the identification of
Gershom as the anonymous lad. The question as to why Rashi
needed to identify the lad at all can be answered by comparing this
section with a similar situation in which Rashi does not utilize a
Midrashic identification. For example, students might be asked to
compare the section in Bamidbar with chapter 24 in Bereishit
dealing with the search for a wife for Yitzchak. The Midrash
identifies Avraham's servant in the story as Eliezer. Rashi, how-

ever, does not identify the servant eventhough the Midrashic identification fits in quite well with the larger context of the Biblical narrative. The perceptive student will note that when the servant is introduced in verse 24:2, the noun is used without the definite article. In contrast, the lad who reports to Moshe is referred to as "הנער", "the lad," utilizing the definite article. If the Torah had stated that "a lad ran", Rashi would not have been compelled to identify him. In other words, the verse in Bamidbar has a textual difficulty that must be solved. In doing so, Rashi utilizes the Midrashic opinion that best fits into the context. In the verse in Bereishit, however, since there is no textual difficulty, Rashi omits the Midrashic identification eventhough it fits in well with the context.

Conclusion

The methodology demonstrated in the above examples can be replicated numerous times throughout the study of Chumash. Nechama believed that by engaging the students in analyses of this sort, they not only internalize more fully both Rashi's commentary and the content of the *Midrashim*, but they also gain an appreciation of the sophistication of Rashi's approach to "פשוטו של מקרא".

CHAPTER IV

USING THE COMMENTATORS:
ASKING THE RIGHT QUESTIONS

Although the study of classical and modern commentaries occu-
pied an important place in Nechama's approach, she did not view it
as an end in itself, but rather as a means to a better understanding
of the text.

> "At the center of the lesson stands the chapter, the verse,
> the story, the law, the issue, the idea. But, on the other
> hand, the commentaries are not extraneous or decorative,
> but they reflect their appellation: they help us to understand
> in depth the chapter, the verse, the issue, and the idea."[1]

It is, thus, important for the teacher to be selective in the use of
Midrashim and commentaries based on their relationship to the
understanding of the text and the goals of the lesson. It is equally
important to ask questions that will guide the student to connect
the commentary to the text. As in the case of questions related
directly to the text, Nechama warned against asking factual questions on the commentaries. Thus, she would oppose the use of
questions such as "What did commentator x or y say on a particular verse?" or "Paraphrase Rashi's commentary on the verse." She
cautioned, as well, regarding the use of appropriately worded
questions that relate solely to the commentaries, but not to the
text.

---

[1] ליבוביץ, נחמה, **לימוד פרשני התורה ודרכים להוראתם**, ההסתדרות הציונית העולמית, תשל״ה, מבוא.

In this chapter, we will examine prototypical questions that Nechama advocated in the analysis of the commentators by looking at a variety of questions on Bereishit 18:1–8:

א. וירא אליו ה׳ באלוני ממרא והוא יושב פתח האוהל כחום היום.

ב. וישא עיניו וירא והנה שלושה אנשים ניצבים עליו וירא וירץ לקראתם מפתח האהל וישתחו ארצה.

ג. ויאמר אדני אם נא מצאתי חן בעיניך אל נא תעבור מעל עבדך.

ד. יקח נא מעט מים ורחצו רגליכם והשענו תחת העץ.

ה. ואקחה פת לחם וסעדו לבכם אחר תעברו כי על כן עברתם על עבדכם ויאמרו כן תעשה כאשר דברת.

ו. וימהר אברהם האהלה אל שרה ויאמר מהרי שלש סאים קמח סלת לושי ועשי עגות.

ז. ואל הבקר רץ אברהם ויקח בן בקר רך ועוב ויתן אל הנער וימהר לעשות אותו.

ח. ויקח חמאה וחלב ובן הבקר אשר עשה ויתן לפניהם והוא עומד עליהם תחת העץ ויאכלו.

1. And the Lord appeared to him (Avraham) in Elonei Mamre, as he sat in the tent door in the heat of the day.
2. And he raised his eyes and looked , and behold, three men stood by him; and when he saw them, he ran from the tent door to meet them, and bowed down to the ground.
3. And he said, my lords, if now I have found favor in your eyes, pass not by, I pray thee, from your servant.
4. Take a little water and wash your feet, and rest yourselves under the tree.
5. And I will fetch a morsel of bread and feed you, and after that you can pass by, because for that reason you came by way of your servant; and they said, may you do as you have spoken."

6. And Avraham hastened to the tent to Sara, and he said: "make ready quickly three measures of meal of fine flour, knead it and make, cakes."

7. And Avraham ran to the herd and fetched a calf tender and good, and he gave it to the youth, and he hurried to prepare it.

8. And he took butter and milk and the calf that he had prepared, and he set it before them, and he stood by them under the tree and they ate.

A. Rashi 18:3 –

ויאמר אדני אם נא וגו׳: לגדול שבהם אמר וקראם כולם אדונים, ולגדול אמר "אל נא תעבור" וכיון שלא יעבור הוא, יעמדו חבריו עמו, ובלשון זה הוא חול (שבועות לה). ד"א קודש הוא, והיה אומר להקב"ה להמתין לו עד שירוץ ויכניס את האורחים. ואע"פ שכתוב אחר: "וירץ לקראתם" האמירה קודם לכן היתה. ודרך המקראות לדבר כן, כמו שפירשתי אצל "לא ידון רוחי באדם" (בר׳ ו, ג), שניתב אחר "ויולד נח את שם את חם..." (ה, לב) ואי אפשר לומר כן אלא הגזירה היתה מקודם עוד כי שנה. ושתי הלשונות בב"ר.

"And he said: 'My lords...'": He spoke to the eminent one among them. He addressed them all as "my lords" אדני, and to the eminent one he said "Do not pass me by, I beg of you" (אל נא תעבור מעל עבדך), since if the eminent one would not pass by, his companions would remain with him. According to this explanation, אדני is secular. Another explanation is that the word is sacred (referring to God) and that he (Avraham) was requesting that the Holy One Blessed Be He wait for him while he ran to take in the travelers. And although this is written after "and he ran toward them, the conversation took place beforehand, and it is the way of the Torah to speak in this manner...."

1. One of the most common questions that Nechama would ask would be: "What difficulty is the commentator addressing?"

Suggested Answer: Rashi is responding to the lack of grammatical consistency between the subject (seemingly plural) and the subsequent verb (singular).

2. Subsequently, one might ask: "How does the commentator solve the problem?"

Suggested Answer: Rashi provides two solutions. In the first solution, Avraham initially addresses all of them, but then addresses the leader of the delegation. In the second solution, Rashi views the subject as referring to God, justifying the use of the singular verb.

3. Nechama held that if Rashi records two explanations (particularly when he connects them with the expression דבר אחר (ד"א or), it indicates that he is not fully satisfied with either one. In such cases, she might ask: "What is the weakness in each of the explanations brought by Rashi?"

Suggested Answer: The weakness of the first explanation is that it does not explain why Avraham subsequently returns to the use of the plural form when he says, "Wash your feet" (ורחצו רגליכם). The weakness of the second explanation is that it creates an inconsistency in the chronological order of the text.

B. 18:3 – Gemara Shabbat 127a:

אמר רב יהודה אמר רב גדולה הכנסת אורחים מהקבלת פני
השכינה דכתיב: ויאמר אדני אם נא מצאתי חן בעיניך, אל נא
תעבור....

36

Rav Yehuda said in the name of Rav, "The mitzvah of hospitality is greater than welcoming the divine presence, as it is written, 'And he said, my lords, if now I have found favor in your eyes, pass not by....'"

Another method utilized by Nechama to compare commentators was to ask whether an additional commentary agreed with a previously learned explanation, or whether it adds an additional explanation. In this case: "Is Rav Yehuda's comments consistent with one of the explanations of Rashi on this verse (see A above), or does he explain it in a different way?"

Suggested Answer: Rav Yehuda is consistent with the second explanation in Rashi.

C. Ramban 18:1 – "And behold three men":

...והנה פירוש הפרשה הזאת, אחרי שאמר כי בעצם היום הזה נמול אברהם (לעיל יז כו), אמר שנראה אליו השם בהיותו חולה במילתו, יושב ומתקרר בפתח אהלו מפני חום היום אשר יחלישנו, והזכיר זה להודיע שלא היה מתכוין לנבואה לא נופל על פניו ולא מתפלל, ואף על פי כן באה אליו המראה הזאת באלוני ממרא, להודיע המקום אשר בו נימול, וזה גילוי השכינה אליו למעלה וכבוד לו, כענין שנאמר במשכן ויצאו ויברכו את העם וירא כבוד ה' אל כל העם (ויקרא ט כג), כי מפני השתדלותם במצות המשכן זכו לראיית השכינה. ואין גלוי השכינה כאן וכאן לצוות להם מצוה או לדבור כלל, אלא גמול המצוה הנעשית כבר....

...And this is the explanation of this section: After it says that Avraham was circumcised on that day, it says that God appeared to him while he was sick from his circumcision, sitting by the door of his tent and cooling off from the heat of the day that weakened him. And it mentions this to in-form us that he did not intend to be involved in prophecy, he didn't bow down and he didn't pray, but nevertheless this vision came to him in Elonei Mamre in order to publicize the place where he was circumcised. And this was a revelation of the Shechina in order to honor him, as it similarly says in the Mishkan (Vayikra 9:23), "And they went out and they blessed the people, and the glory of God appeared to all of the people." – they merited to see the Shechina. And the revelation of the Shechina in both places is not to command a mitzvah or to communicate at all, but a reward for the mitzvah that was already done....

Sometimes Nechama asked an indirect question for the purpose of clarifying the problem in the text and/or the solution of the commentators.

One such question is to have the students justify a proof text brought by the commentator. In this case: "How is our verse similar to the one in Vayikra 9:23 that is quoted by Ramban? What is the common textual difficulty?"

Suggested Answer: In both verses, God appears without any conversation or any apparent purpose. According to Ramban, in both cases, God's appearance is to indicate His approval of the previous action.

D. Rashi 18:5 – "אחר תעברו":

Afterwards, you may go away.   אחר כן תלכו

Nechama held that Rashi and other commentators will comment on a difficult word on its first appearance and not thereafter. If a commentator diverged from this principle, Nechama saw it as an opportunity for a probing question. For example: "Why does Rashi explain the word תעברו in verse 5, but did not comment on the word תעבר in verse 3?"

Suggested Answer: The usage of the word in verse 3 is the normal usage of the word. In verse 5, the word is used in an unusual context. Once a person has spent time in a place, we would tend to say subsequently that he leaves rather than that he passes by.

E. 18:7: Rashi – "אל הנער":

זה ישמעאל לחנכו במצוות

"To the lad": this is Yishmael – to train him in the performance religious commandments.

Similarly, Nechama would question a comment made in one instance that is not repeated in a seemingly similar instance. For example: "Why does Rashi bring the Midrashic identification of the lad in this verse, but does not bring the Midrashic identification of the servant in Bereishit 24:2?"

Suggested Answer: In this verse, the definite article (ה' הידיעה) is used ("the lad"), but in the other case, the definite article is not used. Thus, here the Torah is referring to a specific lad. Rashi adds that the importance of identifying the lad here as Yishmael is that it explains why Avraham would delegate this responsibility, unlike all of the other tasks that he did himself. The character education of his child takes precedence over the drive to perform the mitzvah of welcoming guests himself.

F. 18:5 – Bechor Shor:

כן תעשה כאשר דברת: כלומר כן תעשה תדיר, כאשר דברת
עתה, זהו וייסתך הטוב שאתה מכניס אורחים ומשמשם.

May you do as you have spoken: May you always behave
in such a way as you do now. This is your praiseworthy
custom to invite travelers and offer them hospitality.

Ibn Ezra:

כן תעשה: דרך מוסר, שפת לחם די.

May you do: He was being polite, i.e., a piece of bread will
be sufficient.

A common activity for Nechama involved the comparison of the
opinions of two commentators. For example: "What bothers both
commentators in the verse and what is the difference between their
solutions?"

> *Suggested Answer: In this case there are two difficulties. One difficulty is
> that of extraneous language (לשון יתירה) – if they said "so may you
> do" (ken ta'aseh), why was there a need to add "as you have spoken"
> (ka'asher dibarta)? The second difficulty is not grammatical, but contex-
> tual. The response of the visitors seems to be inappropriate. Given Avra-
> ham's magnanimous hospitality, it seems impolite that the guests are im-
> plying that he may not actually fulfill his promise. Ibn Ezra interprets the
> comment as an attempt to keep Avraham from going beyond what he has
> promised. Bechor Shor sees it as a compliment – "may you always display
> such qualities."*

Sometimes Nechama would try through her question to make the
comparison more focused. For example, she might have asked:

"Compare the interpretations of the phrase 'ka'asher dibarta' according to Ibn Ezra and Bechor Shor." Or alternatively: "What one word could be added to the phrase 'ka'asher dibarta' to make it read like the interpretation of Ibn Ezra and what word could be added to make it read like the interpretation of Bechor Shor?"

Answer: Ibn Ezra – רק *(only)*

Bechor Shor – תמיד *(always)*

G. 18:7: "And Avraham ran to the herd":

רמב"ן: להגיד רוב חשקו בנדיבות כי האדם הגדול אשר היו בביתו שמונה עשר ושלש מאות איש שולף חרב, והוא זקן מאד וחלוש במילתו הלך הוא בעצמו אל אהל שרה לזרז אותה בעשיית הלחם, ואחרי כן רץ אל מקום הבקר לבקר משם בן בקר רך וטוב לעשות לאורחיו.

Ramban: To tell of his great desire for generosity, that such a great man with 318 soldiers in his home, old and weak from his circumcision, went himself to the tent of Sara to encourage her in the making of the bread, and after that ran to the place of the herd to choose a tender and good calf for his guests.

רשב"ם: לפי שאמר להם פת לחם, דבר מועט, לפי שדרכם נחוץ ללכת, הוצרך לרוץ ולמהר, לפי שאמר להם מעט ועשה הרבה.

Rashbam: Because he said to them, "And I will fetch a morsel of bread" because they were in a rush to go, he had to run and hurry, since he said little but did a lot.

In order to connect the commentator to the text, Nechama would at times ask students to find evidence from the text to support the explanation in the commentary. In this case, she utilized this same method to compare the two commentaries: "Find evidence from the text to support the positions of Ramban and Rashbam."

Suggested Answer: The opinion of the Ramban is based on the fact that in the span of six verses (2–7), the verb to run is used twice and the word hurry is utilized three times. The explanation of the Rashbam is based on a comparison of what he said he would do, and what he did. He suggested that he would bring them a little water and a morsel of bread. In the implementation, he brings cakes, butter, milk, and meat.

H. 18:6

In the simple translation of the verse, the phrase קמח סלת is considered to be the construct form and is therefore rendered "meal of fine flour." Rashi and the Gemara, however, interpret it differently.

רש״י: סולת לעוגות קמח לעמילן של טבחים, לכסות את הקדירה....

Rashi: Fine flour (סלת) for cakes, meal (קמח) for the dough used by cooks to coat the pan....

בבא מציעה פז׳ ע״א: כתיב קמח וכתיב סולת. אמר ר׳ יצחק מכאן שהאשה עינה צרה באורחים יותר מן האיש.

Baba Metzia 87a: It says קמח and it says סלת. Rabbi Yitzchak said, "From this we learn that a woman is more stingy with her guests than a man."

Another method that Nechama used for comparing commentators was to ask students to punctuate the verse according to each commentator.

Suggested Answer:
Rashi: Hurry and knead three measures of meal, fine flour, and prepare some loaves.
Rabbi Yitzchak in the Gemara:
    – (Avraham) Hurry and knead three measures of....
    – (Sara) Meal?
    – (Avraham) Fine flour, and prepare some loaves.

Nechama also advocated the practice of having students express their opinions regarding the relative strength of different positions expressed by the commentators, and to bring supporting evidence:

"This method of study has numerous advantages well worth noting. It prompts the students to argument and generates excitement and interest. Considering the chapter according to each different approach forces him to review it several times, accustoms him to delve deeply into the text, and discourages rapid superficial reading. Above all, each student feels that one particular interpretation (depending on his personality and character) is compatible with his sentiments. He is drawn to that interpretation and makes a great effort to convince his friends.... A personal connection is formed between the chapter and the student, he becomes attached to it, it becomes 'his.' In this way our students come to love the Torah and the study of Torah, which is our primary objective."[2]

She rejected the criticism that such an approach can foster a sense of disrespect for the commentators.

"Finally, a reply to the critics who complain that encouraging students to argue over and select commentaries does not educate them to maintain a correct attitude towards our

---

[2] Nechama Leibowitz, *Torah Insights*, Eliner Press, Jerusalem, 1995, p. 155.

teachers and masters... and that further, it is disrespectful for 15–16 year olds to judge them, accepting one and rejecting the other. It seems to me that if all this is done in the proper spirit, the spirit of serious analysis of the commentaries...there is no disrespect. On the contrary, proper regard for scholars consists of studying in depth what they have written. Rashi...would certainly have approved if through studying and analyzing his words students might, at times, come to prefer the explanation of his grandson (Rashbam), or even to agree with his critic, Ramban.... The scholars can receive no greater respect than to have the Torah brought closer to its students as a direct result of what they wrote."[3]

---

[3] Nechama Leibowitz, *Torah Insights*, Eliner Press, Jerusalem, 1995, p. 161.

CHAPTER V

USE OF COMPARATIVE TEXTS: השוואה

Opportunities for Comparison

A methodology that appears quite frequently in Nechama's writings is that of textual comparison. Nechama identified four common situations in which the Torah repeats itself and comparisons can be made:

1. Similar Events
2. Similar Laws or Laws that are Repeated
3. Recapitulations
4. A Command and its Implementation

Presentation to the Students

Comparisons can be presented to students in a variety of ways. Students can be asked in an open-ended fashion to compare two texts. This is effective if the passage is short and the points of comparison are limited. Alternatively, the teacher can direct the students to compare specific items that relate to the lesson. Nechama suggested that a chart be utilized for comparisons of larger sections, particularly if the comparison is complex. Furthermore, the teacher can allow the students to discover discrepancies on their own, or can present them with the comparative information for analysis. These decisions, obviously, depend on the nature of the text being studied and the goals of the lesson.

In the comparison of texts, the students should be sensitized to the following items:

1. Changes in word usage or details surrounding the event or law that is recorded repetitively in the text.
2. Additions of words, phrases, or information
3. Deletions of words, phrases, or information
4. Changes in Order

The purpose of the comparison is not simply to identify the similarities and differences between the two texts, but rather to understand the significance of the differences. Thus, Nechama's questions relating to textual comparison would always focus on the reason for particular changes in the text, or the lessons that can be derived from those changes. In this chapter, we will examine examples of the various formats that allow for comparison.

Formats for Comparison of Texts

1. Similar Events

Events which manifest significant similarities can be better understood by examining their differences. For example, both Avraham and Yitzchak make treaties with Avimelech at Be'er Sheva (Bereishit 21:22–34, 26:13–34). It is interesting to note, however, that Avraham brings a sacrifice after he has concluded the agreement, while Yitzchak brings an offering before negotiating his treaty. Also, both Avraham and Yitzchak give the name Be'er Sheva to the place where the covenant was made, but for different reasons. Avraham names it after the oath that was accepted there by both him and Avimalech, while Yitzchak names it after the well that he dug after the shepherds of Avimelech had closed the wells that Avraham had dug previously. Students might be asked how these differences reflect the different relationships that Avraham and Yitzchak have with Avimelech. Avraham perceives the treaty with Avimelech as a factor that will contribute to his ability to live securely in the land. Yitzchak, however, suffers the duplicity of Avimelech who drives him out of Gerar and whose shepherds continuously struggle with him over the use of wells, including those that were dug by Avraham. Yitzchak realizes that he must establish his own position in the land before negotiating with Avimelech. This is accomplished through the digging of his own well and the bringing of a sacrifice. Only then does he conclude a treaty with Avimelech.

Similarly, the first three events recorded by the Torah in the life of Moshe following his maturation in the house of Paroah all have the same motif (Shemot 2:11–21). In each, Moshe intervenes in an argument that is apparently not related to him. The teacher may ask how the differences between these cases give insight into the personality and value system of Israel's greatest leader. The first struggle is between a Jew and a non-Jew, demonstrating Moshe's concern for the oppression of his people. The second conflict is between a Jew and a Jew, demonstrating Moshe's passion for justice within his own community. In the third conflict, Moshe intervenes in a conflict between non-Jews, demonstrating that the Jewish leader has concern for universal justice as well.

2. Similar Laws or Laws that are Repeated

Similar Laws

As in the narrative sections of the Torah, one finds laws that also exhibit similarities and differences. A classical example is a comparison of the laws governing honor and fear of parents. Both laws govern the relationship between children and their parents. The order in which mother and father are listed in the two command-ments, however, are opposite:

"כבד את אביך ואת אמך..." (שמות כ' י"ב)

"איש אמו ואביו תיראו..." (ויקרא י"ט, ג')

"Honor your father and mother...." (Shemot 20:12)
"A person must fear his mother and his father...."
(Vayikra 19:3)

The teacher should study with the class the differences between honor (כבוד) and fear (יראה) as described in the Gemara (Kid-dushin 31b). Honor is defined as feeding, clothing, and escorting, while fear is demonstrated by not by not sitting in the parent's seat, not standing in his/her place, and not interrupting or disagreeing. One is a close, loving relationship, while the other is a distant relationship of respect. When asked to reflect on the significance of the change in word order, students may arrive at Rashi's under-standing. Rashi indicates that the change in word order reflects the difference in the relationships that normally exist between children and their parents:

רש"י (ויקרא י"ט, ג'): כאן הקדים אם לאב לפי שגלוי לפניו שהבן ירא את אביו יותר מאמו, ובכבוד הקדים אב לאם לפי שגלוי לפניו שהבן מכבד את אמו יותר מאביו, מפני שמשדלתו בדברים.

Rashi (vayikra 19:3): Here the mother is placed before the father because it is revealed before Him (God) that the child fears his father more than his mother, and in the case of honor the father is placed before the mother be-cause it is revealed before Him that the child honors his mother more than his father because she appeases him with words.

Laws That Are Repeated

The Torah repeats in Sefer Devarim many of the laws recorded previously in Shemot and Vayikra. Again, the differences between the renditions can have legal, ethical, and/or philosophical implications. A prime example is the the ten commandments, which appear in both Shemot and Devarim. Commentators have discussed at length the many differences between the two renditions and their significance. We will focus for illustrative purposes on the commandment of shabbat. The most glaring difference between the commandment of shabbat in Shemot and Devarim is the reason given for the mitzvah:

דברים: "וזכרת כי עבד היית בארץ מצרים ויצאך ה' א-להיך משם ביד חזקה ובזרע נטויה על כן צוך ה' א-להיך לעשות את יום השבת". (דברים ה, טו)

שמות: "כי ששת ימים עשה ה' את השמים ואת הארץ את הים ואת כל אשר בם וינח ביום השביעי על כן ברך ה' את יום השבת ויקדשהו". (שמות כ, יא)

Shemot: "For in six days, the Lord made heaven and earth, the sea and all that is in them, and rested on the seventh day. Therefore, the Lord blessed the seventh day and hallowed it." (Shemot 20:11)

Devarim: "And you will remember that you were slaves in Egypt, and that the Lord your God brought you out from there with a mighty hand and an outstreched arm. Therefore, the Lord your God commanded you to keep the sabbath day." (Devarim 5:15)

Furthermore, the commandment as it is worded in Devarim adds the following phrase: "So that your servant and maid servant may rest as well with you."

Clearly, shabbat relates to both the creation of the world and the release from the bondage in Egypt. Students may be asked why one reason is emphasized in Shemot and the other in Devarim? One possibility is that the difference can be understood by taking into account the context in which the commandments were heard. In Shemot, Bnai Yisrael had just left the pagan society of Egypt. It was, therefore, relevant to emphasize the aspect of shabbat relating to creation in order to strengthen the idea that God is the ultimate cause behind all natural phenomena in the world. The commandments in Devarim were delivered by Moshe just before they were about to enter Eretz Yisrael. Here, the emphasis is on social issues such as the treatment of slaves and strangers. As they were about to create a new Jewish society, Moshe highlighted the issues of social justice that are inherent in the commandment of shabbat.

The repetition of laws is found in a number of instances including the returning of lost objects, relieving the burden of an animal, the prohibition of taking interest, and the prohibition of taking a bribe.

3. Recapitulations

The repetition of information in the Torah often takes place through recapitulation, the description by someone of an event that was previously described by the Torah or the transmission of information received by one individual to a third party. A good example of recapitulation is the dream of Paroah that is described by the Torah and is retold by Paroah in his discussion with Yosef. In his reenactment of the dream, Paroah adds comments about the extremely scrawny nature of the thin cows:

תיאור התורה:	שיחזור פרעה:
"והנה שבע פרות אחרות עלות אחריהן מן היאור רעות מראה ודקות בשר..." (בראשית מא, ג)	"והנה שבע פרות אחרות עולות אחריהן דלות ורעות תאר מאד ורקות בשר לא ראיתי כהנה בכל ארץ מצרים לרע...." (בראשית מא, יט) "ותבאנה אל קרבנה ולא נודע כי באו אל קרבנה ומראיהן רע כאשר בתחילה..." (בראשית מא, כא)

The Torah's Description:	Paroah's Reenactment:
"And behold, seven other cows came up after them out of the river, ill favored and lean of flesh…" (Berershit 41:3)	"And behold, seven other cows came up after them from the river, poor and very ill favored and lean of flesh, such as I have never seen in the land of Egypt for badness…" (Bereshit 41:19)
	"And when they [the lean cows] had eaten them [the fat cows] up, it could not be known that they had eaten them, for they were still ill favored as at the beginning." (Bereshit 41:21)

The different approaches of the commentators regarding changes that are found in recapitulations in the Torah are reflected in their explanations on this section. One school of thought, represented by Ibn Ezra, Abarbanel, and Radak, do not attribute significance to such changes. This is expressed in the comment of Radak on verse 41:17:

"וידבר פרעה אל יוסף: כבר כתבנו כי בשנות אדם הדברים
יוסיף או יגרע או ישנה אינו שומר אלא שיהיה ענין אחד, וכן
בספור זה החלום".

"And Paroah spoke to Yosef: We have already written that
a person changes things by adding, subtracting, or changing
words, and is only careful that it expresses the same idea –
and so it was in the telling of this dream."

The other school of thought, represented by Rashi, the Netziv
(Ha'amek Davar), and Samson Raphael Hirsch, do attribute significance to changes in the recapitulation of a passage, claiming that
otherwise, the Torah would not have unnecessarily repeated the
passage:

"ויספר פרעה ליוסף את החלום: אלא משום שיש בהם דברים
שנתחדש שראה גם באיזה דיוקים שלא נתבאר בראשונה ועל כל
דיוק יש פתרון, כאשר יבואר".

"And Paroah told his dream to Yosef: Because there were
new things in them and details that had not been clear in
the first one; and for each detail there is an explanation, as
will be explained." (Ha'amek Davar)

This opinion is strengthened by the fact that when the Torah
records that Paroah told his dream to the Egyptian soothsayers, it
does not repeat the dream:

"...ויספר פרעה להם את חלמו ואין פותר אותם לפרעה".
(בראשית מא, ח)

"And he told them his dream, but there was none who
could interpret it for Paroah." (Bereshit 41:8)

52

Why, then, is the entire dream repeated when he tells it to Yosef? According to Samson Raphael Hirsch, the second rendition of the dream reveals Paroah's emotional reaction to the dream:

> "It is interesting to compare the story of the dream as told by Paroah and the story of the Torah on how the dream was in truth. Above we heard the dream in an objective description, here we see how it is perceived in Paroah's soul."

According to Haketav Vehakabbalah, the changes in the dream have another function. He claims that Paroah's rendition of the dream includes within it, through divine providence, the hints to its solution.

Nechama clearly favored the latter view regarding the significance of changes in repetitive sections of the Torah, for it is the hidden meaning of the recapitualtion that gives textual comparison its pedagogical strength. The discovery of differences, the speculation of possible explanations, and the comparison of the perspectives of classical commentaries are elements which have the power to engage students actively in the learning process. Teachers will be surprised as to how often this methodology can be employed. The following are two more examples:

1. The Garden of Eden:

א-לוהים מצווה את האדם:	חווה מספרת לנחש על הציווי:
"מכל עץ הגן אכל תאכל: ומעץ הדעת טוב ורע לא תאכל ממנו כי ביום אכלך ממנו מות תמות". (בראשית ב' טז—יז)	"מפרי עץ הגן נאכל: ומפרי העץ אשר בתוך הגן אמר א-לוהים לא תאכלו ממנו **ולא תגעו בו** פן תמותון". (בראשית ג, ב—ג)

God's command to Adam:	Chava's retelling of the command to the snake:
"Of every tree of the garden you may freely eat, but of the tree of knowledge of good and evil you shall not eat, for on the day that you eat from it you shall surely die." (Bereshit 2:17)	"We may eat of the fruit of the trees in the garden, but of the fruit of the tree which is in the midst of the garden, God has said that you shall not eat of it **or touch it** lest you die." (Bereshit 3:3)

Rashi records the Midrashic view that the addition of the phrase "or touch it" by Chava played a role in the subsequent events. According to the Midrash, the snake pushed Chava against the tree and demonstrated that she did not die from touching the tree. He then convinced her that she would also not die from eating the fruit. The Midrash demonstrates from this story the importance of the prohibition of adding on to the words of the Torah.

2. Eliezer's Mission: In her *gilyonot*, Nechama presented a lengthy chart detailing the differences between the directions given by Avraham to Eliezer before his departure to find a wife for Yitzchak, and Eliezer's description of his mission to Lavan and Betuel. The following are a few examples:

תיאור אליעזר:	הוראות אברהם:
״לא תקח אשה לבני מבנות הכנעני אשר אנכי ישב בארצו...אל **בית אבי תלך ואל משפחתי**״. (בראשית כד, לז)	״לא תקח אשה לבני מבנות הכנעני אשר אנכי יושב בקרבו : כי אל ארצי ואל מולדתי תלך״. (בראשית כד, ג–ד)
״ה׳ אשר התהלכתי לפניו ישלח	״ה׳ א-להי השמים אשר לקחני

מבית אבי ומארץ מולדתי ואשר
דבר לי ואשר נשבע לי לאמר לזרעך
אתן את הארץ הזאת הוא ישלח
מלאכו לפניך ולקחת אשה לבני
משם״. (בראשית כד, ז)

מלאכו אתך והצליח דרכך ולקחת
אשה **לבני ממשפחתי ומבית
אבי״.**
(בראשית כד, מ)

Avraham's Directive:
"Do not take a wife for my son
from the daughters of the
Caananites among whom I
dwell, but go to my land and to
my birthplace."
(Bereshit 24:3–4)

Eliezer's Description:
"Do not take a wife for my son
from the daughters of the
Canaanites in whose land I
dwell, but go to **my father's
house and to my family.**"
(Bereshit 24:37)

"The Lord, God of Heaven,
who took me from the house
of my father and my birthplace…will send an angel
before you and you shall take a
wife for my son from there."
(Bereshit 24:7)

"The Lord, before whom I
walked, will send an angel with
you and prosper your way, and
you shall take a wife for my son
from **my family and from the
house of my father.**"
(Bereshit 24:40)

Eliezer changes in his description of Avraham's directives any
references that might offend the family. He projects the idea that
Avraham specifically was looking for someone from the family as a
wife for his son. As a result, Eliezer must also change the order of
the events as he recounts his meeting with Rivka:

תיאור אליעזר:
"ואשאל אתה ואמר בת מי את
ותאמר בת בתואל בן נחור אשר ילדה
לו מלכה ואשם הנזם על אפה
והצמידים על ידיה״.
(בראשית כד, מז)

תיאור התורה:
"ויהי כאשר כלו הגמלים
לשתות ויקח האיש נזם זהב
בקע משקלו ושני צמידים על
ידיה עשרה זהב משקלם : ויאמר
יבת מי את?״"
(בראשית כד, כב)

55

The Torah's Description:	Eliezer's Description:
"And it came to pass, as the camels finished drinking, that the man took a golden earring of half a shekel weight, and two bracelets for her hands of ten shekels weight of gold, and said 'Whose daughter are you?'" (Bereshit 24:22)	"And I asked her and said, 'Whose daughter are you?' And she said, 'The daughter of Betuel...' And I put the ring upon her nose and the bracelets upon her hand." (Bereshit 24:47)

Eliezer could not let Lavan and Betuel know that he had decided on Rivka before he knew of her relationship to Avraham. These changes that appear in Eliezer's recapitulation support the ethical principle that it is at times permitted to slightly bend the truth for the sake of peace.

4. A Command and Its Implementation

This format is in practice very similar to recapitulation. It involves the comparison of the implementation of a command to the actual command itself. Often, one finds differences that help to deepen our understanding of the circumstances or the personalities of the individuals involved. An excellent example of this format is Moshe's first visit to Paroah in light of the command that had been given to him by God relating to their first encounter:

ביצוע משה:	ציווי ה':
"וילך משה ואהרון ויאספו את כל זקני בני ישראל: וידבר אהרון את כל הדברים אשר דבר ה' אל משה ויעש האתת לעיני העם... ואחר באו משה ואהרון ויאמרו	"לך ואספת את זקני ישראל... ושמעו לקלך ובאת אתה וזקני ישראל אל מלך מצרים ואמרתם אליו ה' א-להי העבריים נקרה עלינו ועתה נלכה נא דרך שלשת

אל פרעה כה אמר ה׳ א-להי
ישראל שלח את עמי ויחגו לי
במדבר: ויאמר פרעה מי ה׳ אשר
אשמע בקלו לשלח את ישראל לא
ידעתי את ה׳ וגם את ישראל לא
אשלח: ויאמרו: א-להי העברים
נקרא עלינו נלכה נא דרך שלשת
ימים במדבר ונזבחה לה׳ א-להינו
פן יפגענו בדבר או בחרב״.
(שמות ד, כט-ל, ה, א-ג)

ימים במדבר ונזבחה לה׳ א-להינו״.
(שמות ג, טז, יח)

God's Command:

"Go and gather the elders of
Israel together…. And they
shall harken to your voice;
And you shall come, you and
the elders of Israel, to the King
of Egypt and you shall say to
him: 'The Lord, God of the
Hebrews, has met with us;
And now, let us go, we pray
thee, three days journey into
the wilderness that we may
sacrifice unto the Lord our
God.'" (Shemot 3:16, 18)

Moshe's Implementation:

"And Moshe and Aharon went
and they gathered all of the
elders of Israel, and Aharon
spoke all of the words which
the Lord had spoken to Moshe,
and did signs and wonders in
the sight of the people…. After
that Moshe and Aharon came
and said to Paroah: 'Thus says
the Lord, God of Israel: Let my
people go that they may hold a
feast for me in the wilderness.'
And Paroah said: 'Who is the
Lord that I should obey his
voice to let Israel go? I do not
know the Lord and I will not let
Israel go.' And they said: 'The
God of the Hebrews has met
with us. Let us go, we pray thee,
three days journey into the
desert that we may sacrifice to
the Lord our God.'"
(Shemot 4:29–30, 5:1–3)

A comparison of the texts reveals that Moshe did not initially follow the script given to him by God. In his first contact with Paroah, Moshe does not ask to go out to the desert for three days, as God had instructed him. Rather, he demands, in a somewhat prophetic style, that Paroah let his people go. Only after Paroah's flat refusal does Moshe revert to the original plan. Why did Moshe deviate from the plan? It is interesting to note that the classical commentators do not comment on this phenomenon. Nechama suggests that Moshe found himself in an unanticipated difficult situation. The Torah records that Moshe and Aharon came to Paroah. Where were the elders? According to the Midrash, the elders slipped away one by one before arriving at the palace. Thus, Moshe and Aharon found themselves before Paroah as individuals, not as the heads of an official delegation. Nechama claims that Moshe felt unable to negotiate on behalf of Bnai Yisrael without the backing of the elders. He resorted, therefore, to a demand based on the backing of God's authority. When Moshe saw that his modification was ineffective, he reverted to the original plan.

CHAPTER VI

TEXTUAL DIFFICULTIES: קושיות

Introduction

The fact that Nechama often asked questions relating to the
"problem in the text" is based on the fact that many of the classical
commentators were very sensitive to literary deviations in the text
referred to as קושיות. In her book entitled
פירוש רש״י לתורה: עיונים בשיטתו, Nechama in conjunction with
Moshe Arend systematically categorized the קושיות to which Rashi
and other commentators responded. In this chapter, we will examine four examples of קושיות. A list of additional common textual
difficulties is included in Appendix 3.

A. Extraneous Language: לשון יתירה

Perhaps the most prevalent and paradigmatic textual difficulty
encountered in Biblical study is that of extraneous language.
According to a number of the traditional Jewish commentators,
every word of the Torah is significant, and, therefore, any language
that is seemingly extraneous actually has a hidden meaning. Nevertheless, there is not unanimity as to what constitutes extraneous
language. As we have seen in our look at recapitulation and as we
will see in our examination of parallelism, the classical commentators have differing views on this issue. Some are more likely to
accept linguistic convention as an explanation of repetitive language in the text, while others will find extra meaning in every

seemingly repetitive word or phrase. In this section, we will examine three examples of extraneous language.

1. Repetition of Word or Phrases (חזרה מלולית): In most cases, the actual repetition of words or phrases will, according to most commentators, have exegetical meaning. A classical example of this phenomenon is the repetition of the phrase "and the two of them went together" (וילכו שניהם יחדו) in the story of Akeidat Yitzchak:

"ויקח אברהם את עצי העולה וישם על יצחק בנו ויקח בידו את האש ואת המאכלת **וילכו שניהם יחדיו**". (בראשית כב, ו)

"And Avraham took the wood for the offering and placed it upon Yitzchak his son, and he took in his hand the fire and the knife, **and the two of them went together.**" (Bereishit 22:6)

"ויאמר אברהם: א-להים יראה לו השה לעולה בני **וילכו שניהם יחדיו**". (בראשית כב, ח)

"And Avraham said: 'God will show us the lamb for the sacrifice, my son.' **And the two of them went together.**" (Bereishit 22:8)

Rashi explains the repetition as follows:

רש"י כב, ו: "וילכו שניהם יחדיו" אברהם שהיה יודע שהולך לשחוט את בנו היה הולך ברצון ושמחה כיצחק שלא היה מרגיש בדבר.

Rashi 22:6: "And the two of them went together.": Avraham who was going to slaughter his son, and Yitzchak who did not sense anything.

רש"י כב, ח : "וילכו שניהם יחדיו" בלב שוה.

Rashi 22:8: "And the two of them went together": In complete agreement.

According to Rashi, this repetition indicates that the agreement between Avraham and Yitzchak was the same both before and after Yitzchak became aware of his fate.

Another example of the repetition of words is the exhortation to be fruitful and multiply given to Noach at the conclusion of the flood:

"ויברך א-להים את נח ואת בניו ויאמר להם **פרו ורבו** ומלאו את הארץ". (בראשית ט, א)

"And God blessed Noach and his sons and said to them: **'Be fruitful and multiply**, and fill the earth.'" (Bereishit 9:1)

"ואתם **פרו ורבו** שרצו בארץ ורבו בה". (בראשית ט, ז)

"And you shall **be fruitful and multiply**, be abundant in the land and multiply in it." (Bereishit 9:7)

רש"י ט, ז : "ואתם פרו ורבו": לפי פשוטו הראשונה לברכה, וכאן לצווי.

Rashi 9:7: "And you shall be fruitful and multiply": According to the simple meaning, the first was a blessing and the second was a commandment."

2. Repetition of Similar Words or Phrases (מלים נרדפות): The phrase "be fruitful and multiply" (פרו ורבו) is itself an example of

מלים נרדפות, as the two words in the phrase seem synonymous. Some commentators see such expressions as a normal linguistic convention that is found in all languages. An example from modern Hebrew is the expression "איום ונורא", a term used to describe something that is terrible. Nobody would ask a person using that expression to clarify which aspect of their experience was "איום" and which part was "נורא". It is simply a figure of speech that creates emphasis. There are, however, other commentators who see exegetical significance in מלים נרדפות. The following is an example from Rashi's commentary on the phrase "be fruitful and multiply":

רש"י: "ורבו": אם לא אמר אלא פרו היה אחד מוליד אחד ולא יותר, ובא ורבו שאחד מוליד הרבה. (בראשית א, כב)

Rashi: "And multiply": If it only said "be fruitful", each couple would give birth to one and no more. The term "and multiply" comes to indicate that each should have many children. (Bereishit 1:22)

A similar example is found in Bereishit 32:8 describing Yaacov's fear before his encounter with Esav:

"וייִרא יעקב מאד ויצר לו ויחץ את העם אשר אתו ואת הצאן ואת הבקר והגמלים לשני מחנות."

"And Yaacov was very much afraid and frightened, and he divided the people that were with him, and the flocks and the herds and the camels, into two camps."

With regard to this verse, Radak indicates that the repetitive expression is for emphasis and has no other additional meaning. Rashi, on the other hand, does interpret the verse based on the concept of extraneous language:

רד״ק: כפל הענין במלות שונות לרוב יראתו.

Radak: It repeated the issue in different words in order to show the magnitude of his fear.

רש״י: "ויירא ויצר" ויירא שמא ייהרג, ויצר לו אם יהרוג הוא את אחרים.

Rashi: "And he was afraid and he was frightened": And he was afraid that he might be killed, and he was frightened that he might kill others.

3. The Positive and the Negation of Its Opposite

(חיוב ושלילת הפכו): It is common in Biblical poetry to state something positive along with the negation of its opposite, such as "It is darkness and not light" – "חושך ולא אור" (Amos 5:18). Rashi often views such instances as literary style and does not attach additional meaning to the phrase. He does, however, attach significance to the same phenomenon when it appears in prose sections of the Torah. The following description of the pit into which Yosef was thrown by his brothers:

"ויקחהו וישלכו אתו הברה והבור רק אין בו מים".
(בראשית לז, כד)

"And they took him amd threw him into the pit. And the pit was empty, there was no water in it." (Bereishit 37:24)

רש״י: ממשמע שנאמר: והבור רק, איני יודע שאין בו מים? מה תלמוד לומר: אין בו מים, מים אין בו אבל נחשים ועקרבים יש בו".

Rashi: Isn't it understood from the fact that it says that the pit was empty that it had no water in it? It comes to teach us that there was no water in it, but there were snakes and scorpions in it.

Another example is the case of the Egyptian midwives who defied Pharoah's order to kill the Jewish male children:

"וַתִּירֶאןָ הַמְיַלְּדֹת אֶת הָאֱ-לֹהִים וְלֹא עָשׂוּ כַּאֲשֶׁר דִּבֶּר אֲלֵיהֶן מֶלֶךְ מִצְרַיִם וַתְּחַיֶּיןָ אֶת הַיְלָדִים". (שמות א, יז)

"And the midwives feared God and did not do as the king of Egypt had commanded them, and they kept the children alive." (Shemot 1:17)

רש"י: ותחיין את הילדים: מספקות להן מזון.

Rashi: "And they kept the children alive": They gave them food.

In this case, even Ibn Ezra, who usually does not interpret repetitive language, views this as a seemingly extraneous phrase:

אבן עזרא: ותחיין את הילדים: בכל כחן, יותר ממשפטן הראשון.

Ibn Ezra: "And they kept the children alive": With all of their power, more than in the first part of the verse.

The explanations of Rashi and Ibn Ezra are based both on the repetition of the concept, and on the fact that the first usage is passive while the second usage is active.

B. Deviations in Word Order: מוקדם ומאוחר בסדר המלים

Among the most complex and interesting קושיות are deviations in the order of words within a sentence or of events within the narrative. As we will see, the commentators differ in their approaches to deviations in order, and each commentator is not necessarily internally consistent in this regard. As such, deviation from an expected order in the text provides a good opportunity to engage students in interesting textual analysis.

At times, the order of the words within a sentence deviate from our expectation. Expected word order may be based on: 1) chronology, 2) logic, 3) previous usage, or 4) grammatical convention. Commentators deal with deviations in word order in one of the following three ways:

a. By providing an explanation which justifies the deviation.

b. When there is no compelling explanation, by essentially changing the word order. In the classical commentators, this is referred to as a "מקרא הפוך" (inverted verse) or a "מקרא מסורס" (distorted verse). This method appears as the 31st of the "32 Exegetical Principles of Rabbi Eliezer the son of Rabbi Yossi" where it is called "מוקדם שהוא מאוחר בענין". In some ways it is similar to the concept of "אין מוקדם ומאוחר בתורה" (there is no chronological order of sections/*parshiyot* in the Torah) which allows changes in the order of the text when there is a deviation in the chronological order in the narrative (see section on this topic below). It should be noted that when a commentator indicates that a verse is "הפוך" or "מסורס", he is not suggesting an actual textual emendation, but rather that the verse should be understood as if the order of the words was changed.

c. By determining that the apparent deviation is actually justified by the simple meaning of the text ("פשט"). In such cases, no explanation of the word order is indicated. In some instances, this situation will be noted by a commentator, but often it is indicated by the lack of a comment.

In her writings, Nechama Leibowitz brings many examples which demonstrate these approaches to deviations in word order in each of the four above mentioned categories.

1. Chronology

One would expect when discussing members of a family, that they would be mentioned in chronological order (i.e., the father before the son, the older child before the younger child, etc.). When this order is not followed, many commentators deduce additional meaning from the verse. The following are a few examples:

a.

‏"ויען לבן ובתואל..." (בראשית כד, נ)

‏רש"י: "רשע היה וקפץ להשיב לפני אביו".

‏רד"ק: "הקדים לבן לבתואל כי בתואל היה זקן ודברי הבית מוטלים על לבן".

"And Lavan and Betuel answered...." (Bereishit 24:50)

Rashi: "He [Lavan] was evil and jumped to answer before his father."

Radak: "Lavan precedes Betuel because Betuel was old and the management of the house fell on Lavan."

b.

‏"וישלח יעקב ויקרא לרחל וללאה". (בראשית לא, ד)

‏רש"י: "לרחל תחלה ואחר כך ללאה שהיא היתה עיקר הבית".

"And Yaacov sent and he called to Rachel and Leah."
(Bereishit 31:4)

Rashi: "To Rachel and afterwards to Leah because she
[Rachel] was the mistress of the house ["akeret habayit" –
the principle one of the home]."

c.

"ויקברו אתו עשיו ויעקב". (בראשית לה, כט)

רד"ק: "הקדים עשו לפי שהיה בכור ואף על פי שמכר בכורתו,
יעקב היה נוהג בו כבוד ומקדימו לשלום מעת שהשלים אתו".

"And his children Esav and Yaacov buried him (Yitzchak)."
(Bereishit 35:29)

Radak: "Esav went first because he was the first born. And
eventhough he had sold his birthright, Yaacov treated him
with honor and let him go first from the time that he made
peace with him."

d.

"ויקברו אותו יצחק וישמעאל". (בראשית כה, ט)

רד"ק: (בראשית לה, כט): "אבל באברהם... הקדים יצחק
לישמעאל ואף על פי שהיה ישמעאל בכור לפי שהיה יצחק בן
הגבירה וישמעאל בן השפחה".

Radak (in his commentary to 35:29): "By Avraham, Yitzchak went before Yishmael. And eventhough Yishmael was
the first born, Yitzchak was the son of the mistress of the
house, and Yishmael was the son of the maidservant."

רש"י: "מכאן שעשה ישמעאל תשובה והוליך את יצחק לפניו."

Rashi: "From here we see that Yishmael repented and had Yitzchak walk before him."

We can see a pattern of sorts in the methods of Rashi and Radak in dealing with this type of deviation. When Rashi perceives a deviation in chronological order, he brings an explanation that justifies the deviation. In each case, the lack of order relates to the character of one of the individuals mentioned – i.e., the wickedness of Lavan, the importance of Rachel to the household, and the repentance of Yishmael. This is information that is particular to these individuals and that we would not know at this point were it not for the change of order. Rashi does not comment on the verse dealing with Esav and Yaacov because he does not perceive a deviation in this instance since it follows the birth order. Radak, on the other hand, tends to justify the apparent deviation in order, as a manifestation of the simple meaning of the text based on social convention that is not specific to the individuals involved - i.e., the older man is not involved in the management of the house, and the son of the maidservant is not on the same level as the son of the original wife. Only in the case of Esav and Yaacov, which he views as divergent from the other verses, does Radak bring a more exegetical type of explanation that relates to the character of Yaacov.

2. Logic

At times, a verse utilizes a word order that seems inappropriate to the context or to the social or natural order. The following are a few examples:

a.

"ויחלום והנה סלם מצב ארצה וראשו מגיע השמימה והנה מלאכי א-להים עלים ויורדים בו". (בראשית כט, יב)

"And he dreamed, and behold there was a ladder standing on the ground and its top reached to the heaven, and behold angels of God ascended and descended on it." (Bereishit 28:12)

רש״י: עולים ויורדים- עולים תחילה ואחר כך יורדים! מלאכים שליווהו בארץ אין יוצאים חוצה לארץ ועלו לרקיע, וירדו מלאכי חוצה לארץ ללוותו.

Rashi: Ascended and descended – They went up first and afterward went down? The angels that accompanied him in Israel do not go outside of Israel, so they ascended and the angels that were to accompany him outside of Israel descended.

Although as human beings we might conventionally say "ascending and descending," from the perspective of angels who reside on high, the order is different. From this, Rashi deduces that there were angels with Yaacov on earth who first ascended and then others descended. This explanation is consistent with two verses that we find later in Bereishit 32:2–3:

"ויעקב הלך לדרכו ויפגעו בו מלאכי א-להים. ויאמר יעקב כאשר ראם מחנה א-להים זה ויקרא שם המקום ההוא מחנים".

"And Yaacov went on his way, and angels of God met him. And when Yaacov saw them, he said: 'This is God's camp.' And he called the name of that place Machanayim."

רש״י: ויפגעו בו מלאכי א-להים– מלאכים של ארץ ישראל באו לקראתו ללוותו לארץ. מחנים– שתי מחנות: של חוצה לארץ שבאו עמו עד כאן, ושל ארץ ישראל שבאו לקראתו.

Rashi: And angels of God met him – angels of Eretz Yisrael came to meet him and to accompany him in Israel.
Machanayim – Two camps: of chutz la'aretz that accompanied him until now, and of Israel that came to meet him.

Thus, Rashi explains the divergent word order in our verse as well
as two difficult verses that appear later in the text in the same
spirit. Rashbam, on the other hand, sees no problem with the word
order in our verse:

רשב"ם: לפי הפשט אין לדקדק במה שהקדים עולים ליורדים,
שכן דרך ארץ להזכיר עלייה קודם ירידה.

Rashbam: According to the simple meaning there is no
reason to specify why "ascending" comes before "descending," for it is normal to mention ascent before descent.

b. Another example involves a deviation from the natural order:

"ולא שמעו אל משה ויתרו אנשים ממנו עד בקר וירם תולעים
ויבאש ויקצף עליהם משה". (שמות טז, כ)

"But they hearkened not to Moshe, and some of them left
it (the manna) over until morning, and it bred worms and
rotted." (Shemot 16:20)

רש"י: הרי זה מקרא הפוך, שבתחלה הבאיש ולבסוף התליע.

Rashi: This is a "מקרא הפוך" (inverted verse) for first it
rotted and then it became infested with worms.

רמב"ן: הרי זה מקרא הפוך, שבתחלה הבאיש ולבסוף התליע –
לשון רש"י. ואילו היה המן מתליע בדרך הטבע כדרך הטבע
כדרך שאר המתליעים היה הדבר כן, אבל זה שהתליע בדרך נס
יתכן שהרים תולעים תחלה, ואין צורך שנהפוך המקרא.

70

Ramban: "This is a 'מקרא הפוך' for first it rotted and then it became infested with worms" – this is the language of Rashi. If the manna had become infested with worms in a natural way as any other thing, this would be the case. But in this case, where it became infested in a miraculous manner, it is possible that it became infested first, and there is no need to change the order of the verse.

In this case, Ramban explains the apparently divergent word order in the verse as a manifestation of the miraculous nature of the manna. Apparently, Rashi did not find this explanation compelling, and he therefore opts for a change in the word order.

c. A third example of a deviation from a logical word order is found in Bamidbar 27:2 which discusses the appeal of the daughters of Tzlafchad regarding their father's inheritance:

"ותעמדנה לפני משה ולפני אלעזר הכהן ולפני הנשיאם וכל
העדה פתח אהל מועד לאמר: 'אבינו מת במדבר...'"

"And they stood before Moshe, and before Elazar the priest, and before all of the princes and all of the congregation by the door of the tent of meeting, saying: 'Our father died in the wilderness...'"

רש"י: לפני משה: ואחר כך לפני אלעזר? אפשר אם משה לא
יודע אלעזר יודע? אלא סרס המקרא ודרשהו דברי רבי יאשיה.
אבא חנן משום רבי אלעזר אומר בבית המדרש היו יושבים
ועמדו לפני כולם.

Rashi: Before Moshe: And afterwards before Elazar? Is it possible that if Moshe did not know, Elazar would know? But, transpose the verse and explain it [before Elazar and before Moshe], these are the words of Rabbi Yoshiah.

Abba Chanan said in the name of Rabbi Elazar: They were sitting\ in the house of study and they stood before all of them.

Rashi suggests that this is a "מקרא מסורס", as sequential appeals would go from the lower court to the higher court, i.e., not from Moshe to Elazar to the princes, but the opposite. Proper protocol would place Moshe at the end of the verse rather then at the beginning. Rashi, however, also brings an alternative interpretation that obviates the need to change the sentence order. In this interpretation, the daughters of Tzlafchad bring their appeal to all of the authorities at one time. In that case, it would be appropriate to list the participants in descending order of importance. Thus, according to this approach, it is appropriate that the list begins with Moshe. Apparently, Rashi feels that the first interpretation is more compelling, but is hesitant to view it as a distorted verse.

3. Previous Usage

The change of word order in repeating phraseology provides for interpretation that can enrich our understanding of the text, as demonstrated in the following examples:

a. The following verses record the commands given to Noach and his family and their implementation of the commands for both entering and leaving the ark:

"ובאת אל התבה אתה ובניך ואשתך ונשי בניך אתך".
(בראשית ו, יח)

"And you shall come to the ark, you and your sons and your wife and your sons' wives with you." (Bereishit 6:18)

"ויבא נח ובניו ואשתו ונשי בניו אתו ...." (בראשית ז, ז)

"And Noach and his sons and his wife and his sons' wives came..." (Bereishit 7:7)

"צא מן התבה אתה ואשתך ובניך ונשי בניך אתך".
(בראשית ח, טז)

"Go out of the ark, you and your wife and your sons and their wives with you." (Bereishit 8:16)

"ויצא נח ובניו ואשתו ונשי בניו אתו". (בראשית ח, יח)

"And Noach and his sons and his wife and his sons' wives went out." (Bereishit 8:18)

רש"י (ז, ז): "האנשים לבד והנשים לבד לפי שנאסרו בתשמיש המטה, מפני שהעולם היה שרוי בצער".

Rashi (7:7): The women alone and the men alone. From here we learn that they were forbidden to have marital relations because the world was in distress.

רש"י (ח, טז): "איש ואשתו, כאן התיר להם תשמיש המטה".

Rashi (8:16): A man and his wife. Here he permitted them to have marital relations.

From the change in word order, Rashi deduces that conjugal living was prohibited during the flood, but was permitted afterward. Interestingly, Noach and his family exit the ark as they had entered it, men and women separately.

Apparently, they still considered the world to be in a state of distress even after the conclusion of the flood. Rashi recognizes this dynamic in his commentary to Bereishit 9:9 which records

Noach's reaction to God's repeat command to Noach and his
family to procreate (the first time this command was given was
before God's promise not to destroy the world, the second was
after):

רש״י: מסכים אני עמך. שהיה נח דואג לעסוק בפריה ורביב עד
שהבטיחו הקב״ה שלא לשחת את העולם עוד.

Rashi: I [Noach] agree with you, for Noach was worried
about engaging in procreation until God promised not to
again destroy the world.

b. A second example of comparative changes in word order is in
the negotiations between Moshe and the tribes of Reuven and Gad
over their settlement in Trans-Jordan:

״ויגשו אליו ויאמרו גדרות צאן נבנה למקננו פה וערים לטפנו,
ואנחנו נחלץ חשים לפני בני ישראל....״ (במדבר לב, טז)

"And they approached him and they said, **'We will build
sheepfolds here for our cattle and cities for our children,** but we will go ready armed before the Children of Israel." (Bamidbar 32:16)

״(ויאמר אליהם משה...) בנו לכם ערים לטפכם וגדרות לצאנכם....״

"(And Moshe said to them...) **Build cities for your children and folds for your sheep....**" (Bamidbar 32:24)

״ויאמר בני גד ובני ראובן אל משה לאמר עבדיך יעשו כאשר
אדני מצוה: טפנו נשינו מקננו וכל בהמתנו יהיו שם בערי הגלעד,
ועבדיך יעברו כל חלוץ צבא....״ (במדבר לב, כה–כו)

"And the children of Gad and the children of Reuven said
to Moshe saying, 'Your servants will do as my master has

commanded: **our children, our wives, our flocks and all of our cattle** will be there in the cities of Gilad, but your servants will pass over, every man armed for war...."
(Bamidbar 32:25–26)

רש"י (לב, טז): חסים היו על ממונם יותר מבניהם ובנותיהם, שהקדימו מקניהם לטפם, אמר להם משה: 'לא כן, עשו העיקר עיקר והטפל טפל, בנו לכם תחילה ערים לטפכם, ואחר כך גדרות לצאנכם'.

Rashi (32:16): They were more concerned for their money than for their sons and daughters, for they mentioned their cattle before their children. Moshe said to them: "It is not so. Make the essential thing primary and the secondary thing secondary. First build cities for your children and then folds for your sheep."

Here, according to Rashi, the change in word order reflects a conflict of values between Moshe and the two tribes. Thus, Moshe's response is in essence a rebuke that the leaders of the tribes take to heart as reflected in the word order of their final response.

4. Grammatical Convention

From a grammatical standpoint, the word order of a sentence can have a significant impact on its meaning. Nechama gave the following example of two sentences that include the same words, but have very different meanings:

Yesterday they told me that you studied.
They told me that you studied yesterday.

Similar issues arise at times in the Biblical text as demonstrated in the following examples:

a.

"וכל הארץ באו מצרימה לשבר אל יוסף..." (בראשית מא, נז)

"And all of the world came to Egypt to get provisions to Yosef..." (Bereishit 41:57)

רש"י: סרסהו ופרשהו: וכל הארץ באו מצרימה אל יוסף לשבור. ואם תפרשהו כסדרו, היה צריך לכתוב לשבור מן יוסף.

Rashi: Change its order and interpret it: "And all of the world came to Egypt to Yosef to get provisions." And if you wanted to explain it in its original order, it would have to read: "to get provisions from Yosef."

b.

"...בא אלי העבד העברי אשר הבאת לנו לצחק בי" (בראשית לט, יז)

"...he [Yosef] came to me [the wife of Potiphar], the Hebrew servant that you brought to us to mock me." (Bereishit 39:17)

רש"י: בא אלי לצחק בי העבד העברי אשר הבאת לנו.

Rashi: He came to me to mock me, the Hebrew servant that you brought to us.

In these instances, Rashi changes the word order in order to achieve the correct syntax in verses that are clearly not constructed in a correct grammatical fashion. In some instances, the commentators disagree on the meaning of a verse based on its syntax, as in the following examples:

c.

"אתה [לבן] ידעת את אשר עבדתיך ואת אשר היה מקנך אתי. כי
מעט אשר היה לך לפני ויפרץ לרב... ועתה מתי אעשה גם אנכי
לביתי". (בראשית ל, כט–ל)

"You [Lavan] know how I have worked for you and how
your cattle has been with me. For the small amount that
was before me has burst into a large amount. And now,
when will I do **also** ("גם") me for my house."
(Bereishit 30:29–30)

The word "גם" is used to connect the word following it to the
word or phrase immediately before it. Rashi interprets the verse in
the following manner:

רש"י: גם אנכי לביתי, לצורך ביתי, עכשיו אין עושין לצרכי אלא
בני וצריך אני להיות עושה גם אני עמהם לסמכן, וזהו "גם".

Rashi: For the needs of my house. Now nobody is work-
ing for my needs except my children, and I also have to
work with them, and this is the meaning of the word "גם".

Ramban and Radak, however, view this as a "מקרא מסורס" and
change the order of the words:

רמב"ן: מתי אעשה אנכי גם לביתי כאשר עשיתי גם לביתך?

Ramban: When will I work also for my house as I have
done also in your house?

רד"ק: כלומר, מתי אטרח לצרך ביתי כמו שטרחתי בעבורך?

Radak: That is to say, when will I labor for the needs of
my house as I have labored for you?

Ramban explains in his commentary that, although Rashi's explanation is grammatically correct, it cannot be the simple meaning of the text because "we don't find that Yaacov had sheep or that his young children would herd them, since the oldest was 6 years old or less."

A similar situation is found in the following example:

קומו צאו מתוך עמי גם אתם גם בני ישראל ולכו עבדו את ה' כדברכם. גם צאנכם גם בקרכם קחו כאשר דברתם ולכו וברכתם גם אותי". (שמות יב, לא–לב)

"Get up and go out from among my people, you and all of the children of Israel, and go worship God as you said. Take as well your sheep and cattle as you said and go, and bless also ("גם") me. (Shemot 12:32)

רשב"ם: וגם תברכו אותי.

Rashbam: And also bless me.

רש"י: התפללו עלי שלא אמות, שאני בכור.

Rashi: Pray for me that I should not die, since I am a first born.

Rashi implies that as part of their service and prayer to God, they should pray for him as well. According to Rashbam it is a different activity and requires a change in word order. Rashbam states in his commentary on Bereishit 29:30 that "most uses of 'גם' in the Torah are 'הפוכים' (out of order)."

It is interesting that in the last examples, Rashi explains the verse according to its grammatical structure without relying on the concept of "מקרא מסורס", while Ramban, Radak, and Rashbam all change the word order. This is not consistent with their commentaries on other verses. A prime example of the internal inconsistency of commentators with regard to the issue of changes in word order is a comparison of the above commentaries of Rashi and Ramban to Shemot 16:20 and Bereishit 30:30. In the first case, Rashi changes the word order while Ramban interjects a miraculous element into the meaning of the verse in order to justify the original sentence structure. In the latter case, it is Rashi who is unwilling to change the word order while Ramban feels compelled to do so.

At some point, all of the commentators are prepared to change the word order of a verse that they determine to be מסורס or הפוך. It is impossible, however, to determine a consistent pattern in this regard. Thus, each case of difficulties in word order must be analyzed in its own right. It is this analysis that can significantly enhance the students' understanding of the text and the commentaries.

C. Deviation in the Chronological Order of Events in the Narrative

At times, events in the Torah appear to be recorded out of chronological order. Chronological deviations may be indicated by grammatical indicators, such as verb tense, by specific information in the text, or by context. The commentators differ in their identification of the problem and their approaches to solutions.

1. Chronological Changes Indicated by Verb Tense

We encounter our first case of change in chronological order in Rashi's interpretation of Bereishit 4:1:

"וְהָאָדָם יָדַע אֶת חַוָּה אִשְׁתּוֹ וַתַּהַר וַתֵּלֶד אֶת קַיִן...."

"And the man knew ("וְהָאָדָם יָדַע") his wife Eve and she conceived and bore Cain...." (Koren translation)

רש״י: כבר קודם הענין של מעלה קודם שחטא ונטרד מגן עדן, וכן ההריון והלידה, שאם כתב "וידע אדם" נשמע שלאחר שנטרד היו לו בנים.

Rashi: Already before the previous matter, before he sinned and was banished from the Garden of Eden, so too the pregnancy and the birth. For if it had written "and the man knew" ("וַיֵּדַע הָאָדָם"), it would imply that after they were banished before they had children. (Bereishit Rabbah 22:2)

In his commentary on this verse, Rashi reveals a grammatical form that provides an indication that the section is not in its proper chronological order. Rashi is explaining that in Biblical grammar, there are two forms of the past tense, the simple past and the past perfect.

The simple past is usually expressed by use of the וי׳ ההיפוך, the letter vav ("and") that changes the future form of a word into the past tense, and vice versa. An example of this form would be וַיֹּאמֶר מֹשֶׁה translated "and Moshe said." The past perfect is characterized by two distinctions: 1) the verb appears in the form that we recognize in modern Hebrew as the past tense, and 2) the syntax of the verse diverges from the usual format in that the verb follows the subject. Thus, the phrase "וּמֹשֶׁה אָמַר" would be translated according to Rashi as "and Moshe had said." Similarly, Rashi would translate our verse as follows: "And the man had known his wife Eve...."

Thus, according to Rashi, the use of the past perfect indicates that the conception and birth of Cain and Hevel occurred before the banishment from the Garden of Eden. This interpretation negates the concept of original sin advocated by Christianity. The compelling nature of Rashi's approach is strengthened by the fact that the commandment to be fruitful and multiply was given at the time of creation.

In contrast, Ibn Ezra does not agree with Rashi regarding the past perfect form, and views this verse as being in its proper chronological order:

אבן עזרא: כאשר ראה שלא יחיה בגופו בעצמו לעולם הוצרך הוא להחיות המין.

Ibn Ezra: When he realized that he himself would not live forever, he had to give life to the species....

A perfect example of Rashi's approach is found in Shemot 24, where there is an apparent redundancy in the text in that God tells Moshe to ascend the mountain in both verses 1 and 12.

"ואל משה אמר עלה אל ה'..." (שמות כד, א)

רש"י: פרשה זו נאמרה קודם עשרת הדברות, בד' בסיון נאמר לו עלה.

"And to Moshe He said ("אמר"), 'Go up to God....'" (Shemot 24:1)

Rashi: This section was said before the Ten Commandments, on the fourth of Sivan he was told to go up.

"ויאמר ה' אל משה עלה אלי ההרה...." (שמות כד, יב)

רש״י: לאחר מתן תורה.

"And God said to Moshe ("ויאמר ה׳ אל משה"), 'Ascend to Me on the mountain..." (Shemot 24:12)

Rashi: After the giving of the Torah.

According to Rashi, verse 1, which uses the past perfect tense, took place earlier, before the giving of the Ten Commandments. Here, the change in order helps to explain the redundancy in the text.

A third example of Rashi's approach can be found in Bereishit 21:1:

"וה׳ פקד את שרה כאשר אמר...."

"And God had remembered ("פקד") Sarah as He had said (אמר)...."

רש״י: סמך פרשה זו לכאן ללמדך שכל המבקש רחמים על חבירו והוא צריך לאותו דבר הוא נענה תחלה...שפקד כבר קודם שרפא את אבימלך.

Rashi: This section was placed here to teach that one who prays for mercy for his friend and he needs the same thing, he will be answered first.... Sarah conceived before Avimelech was cured.

In this case, the change in chronological order sheds light on an ethical principle that the Torah tries to teach.

2. Chronological Changes Indicated by the Text

The Gemara (Pesachim 6b) introduces the concept: "אין מוקדם ומאוחר בתורה", that there is no chronological order in the Torah, as an exegetical method of dealing with cases of apparent inconsistency when there is not a past perfect verb that serves as an indicator. This concept enables commentators to change the order of the narrative in a similar fashion that the word order of a "מקרא מסורס" verse can be changed. But, how do we know if a particular section is out of order? The example brought in the Gemara is one in which the text itself specifies a change in chronology.

The beginning of Parshat Bamidbar records events that took place on the first day of the month of Iyar, just over one year after the exodus from Egypt:

"וידבר ה' אל משה במדבר סיני באהל מועד באחד לחדש השני
בשנה השנית לצאתם מארץ מצרים לאמר: שאו את ראש כל
עדת בני ישראל...." (במדבר א, א–ב)

"And God spoke to Moshe in the wilderness of Sinai, in the tent of meeting, on the first day of the second month in the second year after they came out of Egypt, saying: 'Take the sum of the congregation....'" (Bamidbar 1:1–2)

In chapter 9 of Bamidbar (Parshat Bahaalotcha), the Torah recounts the commandment to fulfill the Pesach offering, which took place on the first day of Nissan, one month before the events in Parshat Bamidbar:

"וידבר ה' אל משה במדבר סיני בשנה השנית לצאתם מארץ
מצרים בחדש הראשון לאמר: ויעשו בני ישראל את הפסח
במועדו." (במדבר ט, א–ב)

"And God spoke to Moshe in the wilderness of Sinai in the first month of the second year after they came out of Egypt, saying: 'Bnai Yisrael shall keep the Pesach offering at its appointed season.'" (Bamidbar 9:1–2)

In this instance, all of the commentators utilize the concept of "אין מוקדם ומאוחר בתורה". For example, Ramban, who is usually opposed to changing the order of the text, does so in this case:

רמב"ן (טז, ג) : על דעתי כל התורה בסדר זולתי במקום אשר יפרש הכתוב ההקדמה והאיחור, גם שם לצורך ענין ולטעם נכון.

רמב"ן (ט, א) : מכאן אמרו חכמים אין מוקדם ומאוחר בתורה. וטעם האיחור הזה היה כי כאשר בא הספר הזה הרביעי להזכיר המצוות שנצטוו ישראל במדבר סיני לשעתם, רצה להשלים ענין אהל מועד ותקונו כל ימי המדבר.

Ramban (16:3): In my opinion, all of the Torah is in chronological order except in those cases where it explicitly states the change in order, and it is also necessary and for a good reason.

Ramban (9:1): From this instance the Rabbis said that there is no chronological order in the Torah. And the reason for this change of order is that since the fourth book [Bamidbar] comes to teach the commandments that were given to Bnai Yisrael in the desert, it first wanted to complete the matter of the *ohel moed* (tent of meeting) which functioned all of the time that they were in the desert.

According to Ramban, the reason for the change of order here is a common literary convention. While a narrative usually runs in chronological order, at times it may deal with a particular topic in its entirety in one place in order to ensure coherence and relevance.

Rashi, on the other hand, claims that the change in order here teaches an ethical lesson:

רש"י: פרשה שבראש הספר לא נאמרה עד אייר למדת שאין מוקדם ומאוחר בתורה. ולמה לא פתח בזו? מפני שהיא גנותן של ישראל שכל ארבעים שנה שהיו ישראל במדבר לא הקריבו אלא פסח אחד בלבד.

Rashi (9:1): The parsha at the beginning of the book was not said until Iyar, teaching that there is no chronological order in the Torah. Why didn't it start with this [the Pesach]? Because it was a disgrace to Bnai Yisrael that they only celebrated this Pesach during their 40 years in the desert.

Thus, according to Rashi, by means of this change in order, the Torah models moral sensitivity.

3. Chronological Changes Indicated by the Context

Most cases of "אין מוקדם ומאוחר בתורה", however, are not indicated by the text or by the verb tense. As indicated previously, Ramban refrains from changing the chronological order in such cases. Others, however, do utilize the concept of "אין מוקדם ומאוחר בתורה" when they feel that it is warranted by the context. Interestingly, they often disagree as to when the concept should be applied. A comparative look at a number of cases in which at least one commentator employs the concept "אין מוקדם ומאוחר בתורה" will help us to further understand the criteria utilized in determining chronological order.

An example of this is found in Shemot 31:18:

"ויתן אל משה ככלתו לדבר אתו בהר סיני שני לחת העדת...."

"And when he finished speaking with him on Mt. Sinai, He gave Moshe the two tablets of testimony..."

רש״י: אין מוקדם ומאוחר בתורה. מעשה העגל קודם לציווי מלאכת המשכן.

Rashi: There is no chronological order in the Torah אין מוקדם ומאוחר בתורה. The sin of the calf came before the command to build the mishkan.

Rashi's use of "אין מוקדם ומאוחר בתורה" in this case is tied to his belief that the command to build the mishkan was a direct result of the sin of the golden calf. The mishkan, the symbol of God's continued presence in the camp, is in Rashi's view the solution of the problem that led to the sin of the calf. Ramban contends that the building of the mishkan was intended a priori as a value unto itself, unrelated to the sin of the calf.

There are cases in which Rashi does not change the order of the text while others employ "אין מוקדם ומאוחר בתורה". For example, in Shemot 18:1, Rashi maintains the order of the text while Ibn Ezra employs "אין מוקדם ומאוחר בתורה":

"וישמע יתרו כהן מדין חתן משה את כל אשר עשה א-להים למשה ולישראל...."

"And Yitro the Priest of Midian, the father-in-law of Moshe, heard everything that God did to Moshe and His people Israel...."

רש״י: מה שמועה שמע ובא, קריעת ים סוף ומלחמת עמלק.

Rashi: What things did he hear and come? The splitting of the sea and the war with Amalek. (Mechilta)

אבן עזרא: לפי דעתי שיתרו בא אל משה אחר שבנה המשכן.

Ibn Ezra: In my opinion, Yitro came to Moshe after he had erected the *mishkan.*

In this case, Rashi follows the Midrashic understanding that the verse is referring to the splitting of the sea and the war with Amalek. Ibn Ezra, who relies less on *Midrashim* than Rashi, is convinced that this approach is inconsistent with the continuation of the chapter that refers to sacrifices and to God's laws and teachings ("את חוקי הא-לקים ואת תורותיו"). According to Ibn Ezra, these elements were not revealed until the giving of he Torah. Thus, he concludes that this section regarding Yitro actually took place later in Shemot.

In the following example, as well, Ibn Ezra utilizes the concept of "אין מוקדם ומאוחר בתורה", while Rashi and Ramban do not:

"ויקח קורח בן יצהר בן קהת בן לוי ודתן ואבירם בני אליאב ואון בן פלת בני ראובן... ויקהלו על משה ועל אהרן ויאמרו אליהם רב לכם כי כל העדה כלם קדשים ובתוכם ה' ומדוע תתנשאו על קהל ה'." (במדבר טז, א–ג)

אבן עזרא: זה הדבר היה במדבר סיני כאשר נתחלפו הבכורים ונבדלו הלווים כי חשבו ישראל שמשה אדונינו עשה מדעתו לתת גדולה לאחיו...

"And Korach the son of Yitshar, the son of Kehat, the son of Levi, and Datan and Aviram the sons of Eliav, And On the son of Pelet of the sons of Reuven took men... and they gathered themselves together against Moshe and Aharon, and said to them: "You take too much upon you, seeing that all of the congregation are holy, and God is among them. Why then do you raise yourself above the congregation of the Lord." (Bamidbar 16:1–3)

Ibn Ezra: This thing took place in the Desert of Sinai when the first born were replaced by the Levites, because Israel thought that our master Moshe did it of his own volition, in order to give stature to his brother....

Ibn Ezra contends that the rebellion of Korach was motivated by suspicions that Moshe was usurping power for his own family, as reflected in the appointment of the sons of Aharon as the priests. If so, in his opinion, the event logically took place at the time that the appointment was made.

Rashi and Ramban agree that Korach was motivated to rebel by the appointment of Aharon's family as the priests as well as the appointment of Eltzafon as the leader of the tribe of Levi, but they do not utilize the concept of "אין מוקדם ומאוחר בתורה" in order to change the chronology of the text. Ramban explains that Korach did not implement the rebellion immediately, but waited until the time was ripe to recruit others to the cause:

רמב"ן: וזה מדעתו של רבי אברהם שהוא אומר במקומות רבים אין מוקדם ומאוחר בתורה לרצונו.... אבל היה הדבר הזה במדבר פראן בקדש ברנע אחר מעשה המרגלים.... והנה ישראל בהיותם במדבר סיני לא אירע להם שום רעה כי גם בדבר העגל שהיה החטא גדול ומפורסם היו המתים מועטים ונצלו בתפילתו של משה שהתנפל עליהם ארבעים יום וארבעים לילה, והנה היו אוהבים אותו כנפשם ושומעים אליו, ואילו היה אדם מורד על משה בזמן ההוא היה העם סוקלים אותו.

ולכן סבל קרח גדולת אהרן... אבל בבואם אל מדבר פראן ונשרפו באש התבערה ומתו בקברות התאוה רבים וכאשר חטאו במרגלים לא התפלל משה עליהם ולא בטלה גזירה מהם ומתו נשיאי כל השבטים במגפה לפני ה' ונגזר על כל העם שיתמו במדבר ושם ימותו, אז היה נפש כל העם מרה והיו אומרים בלבם כי יבואו להם בדברי משה תקלות, ואז מצא קרח מקום לחלוק על מעשיו וחשב כי ישמעו אליו העם.

Ramban: And this is opinion of R. Avraham [Ibn Ezra] who says in many places that there is no chronological order in the Torah as he pleases.... But this took place in the Desert of Paran in Kadesh Barnea after the incident of the spies.... And behold nothing bad happened to Israel when they were in the Desert of Sinai, for even in the incident of the calf which was a great sin, the number that died was small, and they were saved by the prayers of Moshe who interceded for then for forty days and forty nights. And they therefore loved him as themselves and obeyed him – and if anyone would have rebelled against Moshe at that time, the people would have stoned him.

Therefore, Korach tolerated the increased stature of Aharon... But when they came to the Desert of Paran and were burned in the fire of Taverah, and many died at Kivrot Hataavah, and Moshe did not pray on their behalf when the spies sinned and the decree was not nullified, and the princes of all of the tribes died in a plague, and God decreed that all of the people would die in the desert, then the people were bitter because Moshe brought upon them difficulties. Then Korach found the opportunity to disagree with his actions, and thought that the people would listen to him.

Ramban objects to the subjective manner in which Ibn Ezra, and in some instances Rashi, make use of the concept "אין מוקדם ומאוחר בתורה". He refrains from utilizing "אין מוקדם ומאוחר בתורה" unless it is objectively indicated by the text. It is, in fact, the subjective nature in which this concept is employed that provide excellent pedagogical opportunities for Tanach instruction through deviations in the chronological order of the narrative. The range of criteria indicating the need for changes in order, the variance in the opinions of the commentators, and the internal inconsistency within the commentaries, enable the teacher to engage the students in interesting textual analysis and comparative study of the commentators that will deepen his/her understanding of the text, the commentaries, and the values that they endeavor to transmit.

D. Lack of Internal Consistency: סתירות ואי התאמה

Inconsistency within a verse or a section can take the form of a lack of grammatical agreement or lack of uniformity in content.

The following are three common examples of קושיות based on inconsistency.

1. Grammatical Inconsistency

A common textual inconsistency that allows for exegesis is grammatical inconsistency within the verse or within a clearly defined section of the Torah. This may take the form of a lack of agreement between the subject and the verb or between a noun and an adjective with regard to number or gender, as in the following example from Shemot 3:5:

ויאמר אל תקרב הלם של נעליך מעל רגליך כי המקום אשר אתה
עומד עליו אדמת קודש הוא.

And He said: "Put off your shoes from upon your feet for the place whereon you stand is holy ground."

Rashi: Is Holy Ground: The Place (המקום)

The problem to which Rashi is reacting is the lack of agreement between "ground" (אדמה) which is feminine and "is" (הוא) which is masculine. He solves the difficulty by indicating that the word

90

הוא is actually defining the word "place" (המקום), which is masculine, and which appears earlier in the verse.

A similar difficulty is an unexpected change in number or gender within a verse, as in Shemot 19:2:

"**ויסעו** מרפידים **ויבאו** מדבר סיני **ויחנו** במדבר **ויחן** שם ישראל נגד ההר."

"**And they traveled** from Refidim **and they came** to the Desert of Zin **and they camped** in the desert, and Yisrael **camped [singular]** there opposite the mountain."

רש"י: ויחן שם ישראל: כאיש אחד בלב אחד אבל שאר כל החניות בתרעומות ובמחלוקת.

Rashi: "And Yisrael camped there": as one person with one heart, but all of the other encampments were with resentment and argument.

From the use of the singular verb "ויחן" after several plural verbs, Rashi learns that Bnai Yisrael were uniquely united as they stood to receive the Torah.

2. Lack of Uniformity

Lack of internal consistency relating to content presents a קושיה only when seen in the context of the entire section because it deviates from an expectation based on previous usage. The following example from the third chapter in Bereshit is a classical example:

In the story of the Garden of Eden, a sin is committed that involves three perpetrators, Adam, Chava, and the serpent. To Adam and Chava, He addresses a question regarding their role in the incident:

ויאמר: "מי הגיד לך כי עירום אתה המן העץ אשר צויתיך
לבלתי אכל ממנו אכלת?" (בראשית ג, יא)

And He said [to Adam]: "Who told you that you are naked? Did you eat from the tree from which I commanded you not to eat?" (Bereishit 3:11)

ויאמר ה' א-להים לאשה: "מה זאת עשית?" (בראשית ג, יג)

And God said to Chava: "What is this you have done?" (Bereishit 3:13)

To the snake, however, God does not address a question. Rather, He issues a definitive statement:

ויאמר ה' א-להים אל הנחש כי עשית זאת ארור אתה מכל
הבהמה ומכל חית השדה על גחנך תלך ועפר תאכל כל ימי
חייך." (בראשית ג, יד)

And God said to the serpent: "Because you did this, you will be cursed from among all of the cattle and the beasts of the field; you shall go on your belly and you shall eat the dust all the days of your life." (Bereishit 3:14)

רש"י: כי עשית זאת: מכאן שאין מהפכים בזכותו של מסית,
שאילו שאלו למה עשית זאת, היה לו להשיב: דברי הרב ודברי
התלמיד דברי מי שומעין.

Rashi: Because You Did This: From here we learn that one does not intercede in favor of an instigator. For had He asked him, "Why have you done this?"he would have been able to answer, "The words of the teacher and the words of the student, whose words should one heed [i.e., Adam and Chava should have listened to God and not the serpent]."

Rashi indicates that God changed his approach with the serpent because in a strict legal sense, he had less culpability than Adam and Chava. By changing the manner in which the serpent was addressed, the Torah expresses that the serpent has a high level of accountability for this incident.

Another example of lack of uniformity is found in the first chapter of Bereishit:

"ויהי ערב ויהי בקר יום **אחד**" (א, ה)

"ויהי ערב ויהי בקר יום שני" (א, ח)

"ויהי ערב ויהי בקר יום שלישי" (א, יג)

"ויהי ערב ויהי בקר יום רביעי" (א, יט)

"ויהי ערב ויהי בקר יום חמישי" (א, כב)

"ויהי ערב ויהי בקר יום **הששי**" (א, לא)

"And it was evening and it was morning, **day one**." (1:5)

"And it was evening and it was morning, [the] second day." (1:8)

"And it was evening and it was morning, [the] third day." (1:13)

"And it was evening and it was morning, [the] fourth day." (1:19)

"And it was evening and it was morning, [the] fifth day." (1:22)

"And it was evening and it was morning, **the** sixth day." (1:31)

רש"י: יום אחד... למה כתב אחד? לפי שהיה הקב"ה יחיד בעולמו שלא נבראו המלאכים עד יום שני. יום הששי: הוסיף ה' בששי בגמר מעשה בראשית, לומר שהתנה עמהם על מנת שיקבלו עליהם ישראל חמשה חומשי תורה.

Rashi: One Day: ...why did he write one (אחד) instead of first (ראשון)? Because the Holy One Blessed Be He was the only being in the world, for the angels were not created until the second day. The Sixth Day: The text adds the letter ה to the word שישי at the completion of the work of creation to indicate that He stipulated with them [His creations, that they would remain in existence] on condition that Israel would accept the five (ה) books of the Torah....

In these two commentaries, Rashi is relating to two inconsistencies in the numbering of the days of creation:

a. On the first day, the cardinal number "one" is used, while on the other days the ordinal numbers (second, third, etc.) are used. According to Rashi this indicates that only on the first day did God exist alone in the world.

b. Only on the sixth day did the Torah use the definite article ה, "the." According to Rashi this refers to the five books of the Torah as a necessary condition of creation. Similarly, Rashi offers an alternative explanation that it refers specifically to the sixth day of Sivan, the day on which the Torah would be given.

3. Conflicting Information

One of the most challenging aspects of Torah study is the reconciliation of seemingly contradictory sections. The following are two examples of this phenomenon with two paradigmatic solutions commonly used by the commentators:

a. The first two chapters of Bereishit present two seemingly different versions of the creation of the world. For example, the description of the creation of mankind in chapter 1 seems to contradict the description in chapter 2:

"וייצר ה' א-להים את האדם עפר מן   "ויברא א-להים את האדם
האדמה ויפח באפיו נשמת חיים ויהי   בצלמו בצלם א-להים ברא
האדם לנפש חיה ויטע ה' א-להים גן   אתו זכר ונקבה ברא אתם."
בעדן מקדם וישם שם את   (א, כז)
האדם אשר יצר..." (ב, ז–ח)

"And God created man in His image, in the image of God he created him; male and female he created them." (1:27)	"And the Lord God formed man of the dust of the earth, and breathed into his nostrils the breath of life, and man became a living soul. And the Lord God planted a garden eastward in Eden, and there he put the man whom he had formed...." (2:7–8)

Rashi is concerned by the fact that the Torah had already described the creation of man previously. Furthermore, there are a number of discrepancies between the two descriptions including whether man was created ex nihilo or formed from existing matter. Rashi utilizes the principle of כלל שלאחריו מעשה (a generalization followed by a specification) to explain the apparent contradictions:

רש"י: מקדם: ראיתי בברייתא של ר' אליעזר בנו של ר' יוסי הגלילי מל"ב מדות שהתורה נדרשת וזו אחת מהן: כלל שלאחריו מעשה הוא פרטו של ראשון. (ב, ח)

Rashi: "Eastward": I saw in the braita of R. Eliezer the son of R. Yossi Haglili of the 32 midot [exegetical techniques] that explain the Torah, and this is one of them: a general statement followed by an act (כלל שלאחריו מעשה), it [the act] is a specification of the first. (2:8)

In Bamidbar 11:4-6, the Torah describes the complaints of Bnai Yisrael with regard to the manna that was provided to them as food in the desert:

״ויבכו גם בני ישראל ויאמרו מי יאכלנו בשר? זכרנו את הדגה
אשר נאכל במצרים חנם... ועתה נפשנו יבשה אין כל בלתי אל
המן עינינו״.

"And the Children of Israel wept again and said: Who shall
give us meat? We remember the fish that we ate freely in
Egypt... but now our soul is dried away, there is nothing at
all before our eyes but this manna."

The text continues in verses 7–8:

״והמן כזרע גד הוא ועינו כעין הבדלח. שטו העם ולקחו וטחנו
ברחים או דכו במדוכה ובשלו בפרור ועשו אתו עגת והיה אעמו
כטעם לשד השמן. ״

"And the manna was like coriander seed, and its color was
like the color of bdellium. And the people went about and
gathered it, and ground it in mills or beat it in a mortar, and
boiled it and made cakes of it, and the taste of it was like
the taste of oil cakes."

The latter two verses speak in praise of the manna, in contradiction
to the sentiments expressed earlier. Rashi explains the apparent
contradiction by using the concept of מי שאמר זה לא אמר זה, that
although no change of speakers was indicated, the actual statement
of the Children of Israel ends at the end of verse 6. Rashi attributes
the subsequent text to God.

The preceding examples are only a few illustrations of internal
inconsistencies within the text. The apparent contradictions that
occur throughout the Torah provide excellent opportunities to
develop the analytical skills of the students and to enrich the text
with creative solutions.

Conclusion

The textual difficulty (קושיה) is a critical element of Biblical exegesis. In concluding this section, it is appropriate to cite a discussion of the nature of the קושיה that Nechama related to the four questions in the Pesach seder:[1]

The Four Questions – ארבעה הקושיות

Nechama liked to refer to the four questions to demonstrate the difference between a קושיה and a שאלה. The four questions, she pointed out, are referred to as the ארבעה קושיות rather than the ארבעה שאלות. This is based on the way in which the questions are framed. Each of the four questions follows the same format:

On all other nights we _____ , but tonight we _____ .

According to Nechama, this format represents a קושיה, as opposed to the simple שאלה format which would be:

Why on this night do we _____ ?

The שאלה is a simple informational question. The קושיה, on the other hand, takes note of something that deviates from the norm, from something that we expect based on previous knowledge or experience. It is, thus, a sharper question that requires a more specific answer. The קושיה is the fundamental pedagogic instrument of both the Pesach seder and of Biblical exegesis. Nechama's insight turns what many think of as the child's part of the seder ritual into a sophisticated paradigm for Torah learning.

---

[1] As told by Yitshak Reiner in *Studies on the Haggadah from the Teachings of Nechama Leibowitz*, Urim Publications, Jerusalem, 2002, pp. 28–29

CHAPTER VII

BIBLICAL LITERARY STYLE: סגנון

In her *gilyonot*, Nechama at times included a section entitled
שאלות סגנון, designed to help students analyze stylistic features of
the Biblical text. A sensitivity to these nuances can help students
gain a greater understanding of emotional issues in the narrative or
to uncover addition levels of meaning in the text. The following are
several examples of Biblical literary style:

A. The Key Word: המלה המנחה

A prominent stylistic approach in Nechama's methodology is the
analysis of key words or phrases.[1] The key word is an expression
that is used repetitively in a particular section of the Torah. According to Nechama, this repetition has exegetical significance. A
classical example of a key word is found in Bereishit 18:2–7 which
we analyzed in Chapter 4. This section, dealing with Avraham's
hospitality to the angels, utilizes forms of the words "run" (רץ) and
"hurry" (מהר) 5 times in this short section. These words hint to us
that the message of this section relates to Avraham's zealous
approach to welcoming guests.

---

[1] This concept is discussed in detail by Martin Buber in **דרכו של מקרא**, Bialik
Institute, Jerusalem, 1964, pp. 300–307.

Another interesting example of the key word is found in Devarim
26:1–11:

1) והיה כי תבוא אל הארץ אשר ה' א-להיך **נתן** לך נחלה
וירשתה וישבת בה.

2) ולקחת מראשית כל פרי האדמה אשר תביא מארצך אשר ה'
א-להיך **נתן** לך ושמת בטנא והלכת אל המקום אשר יבחר ה'
א-להיך לשכן שמו שם.

3) ובאת אל הכהן אשר יהיה בימים ההם ואמרת אליו הגדתי
היום לה' א-להיך כי באתי אל הארץ אשר נשבע ה' לאבתינו
לתת לנו.

4) ולקח הכהן הטנא מידך והניחו לפני מזבח ה' א-להיך.

5) וענית ואמרת לפני ה' א-להיך ארמי אבד אבי וירד מצרימה
ויגר שם במתי מעט ויהי שם לגוי עצום ורב.

6) וירעו אתנו המצרים ויענונו **ויתנו** עלינו עבודה קשה.

7) ונצעק אל ה' א-להי אבתינו וישמע ה' את קלנו וירא את ענינו
ואת עמלנו ואת לחצנו.

8) ויצאנו ה' ממצרים ביד חזקה ובזרע נטויה ובמרא גדל
ובאתות ובמפתים.

9) ויבאנו אל המקום הזה **ויתן** לנו את הארץ הזאת ארץ זבת
חלב ודבש.

10) ועתה הנה הבאתי את ראשית פרי האדמה אשר **נתתה** לי ה'
והנחתו לפני ה' א-להיך והשתחוית לפני ה' א-להיך.

11) ושמחת בכל הטוב אשר **נתן** לך ה' א-להיך ולביתך אתה
והלוי והגר אשר בקרבך.

1) And it shall be when you come into the land which
the Lord your God **gives** to you as an inheritance, and you
possess it and dwell in it.

2) And you shall take of all of the fruit of the earth that
you shall bring from your land that the Lord your God
gives to you, and you shall put it in a basket and go to the
place that the Lord your God shall choose to place His
name there.

3) And you shall go to the priest that shall be in those days, and say to him: "I profess this day to the Lord your God that I have come to the land that God swore to our fathers to **give** to us."

4) And the priest shall take the basket from your hand, and place it before the altar of the Lord your God.

5) And you shall answer and say before the Lord your God: "My father was a wandering Aramean, and he went down to Egypt, and he sojourned there, few in number, and became there a nation, great, mighty, and numerous.

6) And the Egyptians dealt ill with us, and they **gave** to us hard labor.

7) And we cried out to God, the God of our fathers, and God heard our voice, and He saw our affliction, and our labor, and our oppression.

8) And God took us out of Egypt with a strong hand, and an outstretched arm, and with great awe, and with signs, and with wonders.

9) And He brought us to this place, and He **gave** us this land, a land flowing with milk and honey.

10) And now behold I have brought the first fruit of the ground that you, O God have **given** me," and you shall place it before the Lord your God, and bow down before the Lord your God.

11) And you shall rejoice in all of the good that the Lord your God has **given** to you and your household, you and the Levi and the stranger that is in your midst.

In this section, forms of the word "give" (נתן) appear seven times in the text. Not only is the word used repeatedly, but it creates a particular pattern. The first three and last three usages refer to God's graciousness to Bnai Yisrael. The fourth usage, which falls in the middle of the six other usages, refers to the hard work given by the Egyptians to Bnai Yisrael. This pattern emphasizes that God is the provider of all good, as opposed to the oppression that has been meted out to the Jewish people by the nations of the world throughout history.

A third example of the key word involves the repetition of God's name which occurs in three places in the Torah: Bereishit 25–32 dealing with Yosef's analysis of Pharoah's dreams, Shemot 2:23–25 relating to the cries of Bnai Yisrael to God as a result of the increased Egyptian oppression, and Bamidbar 32:20–23 regarding the negotiations between Moshe and the tribes of Gad and Reuven over their settlement in the transjordan area.

ויאמר אליהם משה: אם תעשון את הדבר הזה אם תחלצו **לפני ה'** למלחמה ועבר לכם כל חלוץ את הירדן **לפני ה'** עד הורישו את אויביו מפניו ונכבשה הארץ **לפני ה'** ואחר תשבו והייתם נקים **מה'** ומישראל והיתה הארץ הזאת לכם לאחזה **לפני ה'**. (במדבר לב, כ–כג)	ויהי בימים הרבים ההם וימת מלך מצרים ויאנחו בני ישראל מן העבודה ויזעקו ותעל שועתם אל **הא-להים** מן העבודה וישמע א-**להים** את נאקתם ויזכור א-**להים** את בריתו את אברהם את יצחק ואת יעקב וירא א-**להים** את בני ישראל וידע א-**להים**. (שמות ב, כג–כה)	ויאמר יוסף אל פרעה: חלום פרעה אחד הוא את אשר **הא-להים** עשה הגיד לפרעה...הוא הדבר אשר דברתי אל פרעה אשר **הא-להים** עשה הראה את פרעה...ועל השנות החלום אל פרעה פעמים כי נכון הדבר מעם **הא-להים** וממהר **הא-להים** לעשותו. (בראשית מא, כה, כח, לב)
And Moshe said to them: "If you will do this thing, if you will go armed **before the Lord** to war, and will go all of you armed **before the Lord,** until He has driven	And it came to pass in the course of those many days that the king of Egypt died, and Bnai Yisrael sighed because of the bondage, and they cried and their cry rose up to **God**	And Yosef said to Pharoah: "The dream of Pharoah is one – **God** has declared to Pharoah what he is about to do."...This is the thing that I have spoken to Pharoah: What **God** is about to

do he has shown to Pharoah....As for the repitition of the dream to Pharoah twice, it is because the thing is fast determined by **God,** and **God** will shortly bring it to pass. (Bereishit 41:25, 28, 32)

because of the bondage. And **God** heard their groaning, and **God** remembered his covenant with Avraham, Yitzchak, and Yaacov. And **God** looked upon Bnai Yisrael, and **God** apprehended. (Shemot 2:23–25)

out His enemies before Him, and the land be subdued **before the Lord,** then afterward you will return and be guiltless **before the Lord** and before Israel, and this land shall be your possession **before the Lord.** (Bamidbar 32:20–23)

In all three cases, the repitition of God's name indicates a turning point with regard to the recognition of God and His role in history. In Bereishit, Yosef repeats God's name in order to impress upon Pharoah that it is God rather than Yosef who is the interpreter of the dreams. The section in Shemot reflects the recognition on the part of Bnai Yisrael that their salvation will come from God. At this point they cry out sincerely to God, and God hears their cry. And in Bamidbar, the repetition of the phrase "before God" (לפני ה') brings the tribes of Gad and Reuven to realize that they must fight for Eretz Yisrael out of commitment to God, and not just out of commitment to their brothers. In all three instances, that which was previously considered to be a human process, is now recognized as a divinely initiated plan.

B. What's In a Name?

One feature of Biblical literary styles relates to the way in which an individual can be called by a variety of names, titles, or descriptive words within a particular section of the Torah. A comparison and

analysis of the references often demonstrates different relationships between the individual and the other players in the story.
Students can be asked to speculate on the significance of the
different appellations. The following are several examples of this
phenomenon:

1. In the story of Hagar and Yishmael in chapter 21 of Bereshit,
Yishmael is referred to differently from the perspective of each of
the participants in the event:

> **a.** Sarah – "The Son of Hagar" (בן הגר) or "The Son of the
> Maidservant" (בן האמה)
> **b.** Avraham – "His Son" (בנו)
> **c.** Hagar – "The Child" (הילד)
> **d.** The Torah (God) – "The Youth" (הנער)

The expression "The Youth" is the objective term utilized in the
narrative. Sarah uses two expressions that both identify Yishmael
as an outsider, the son of Hagar. These terms seem to delegitimize
Yishmael's connection to the legacy of Avraham. Avraham, on the
other hand, views Yishmael as "his son," a warm reference that
reflects the tension between Sarah and Avraham on the issue of
Yishmael's place in the home. From Hagar's perspective, Yishmael
is referred to as "the child," one who is younger than a "youth." In
the eyes of a mother, her son is always a child. The term as used
here, however, also connotes a sense of distance. Unlike Avraham
who views Yishmael as **his** son, Hagar sees him as **the** child, not
her child. This detached relationship is reflected in the subsequent
events, when Hagar leaves the dying child under the tree rather
than holding him.

2. In a similar example, Yosef is referred to in a variety of ways in
Bereshit 37:18-32, the story of his kidnapping and sale. At the
beginning of the story, the brothers as a group refer to Yosef as
"the dreamer" (בעל החלומות), an obviously negative appellation

from their perspective. At the end of the story, when they bring Yosef's bloody coat to their father, they refer to Yosef as "your son" בנך. All other references to Yosef by the brothers throughout the story utilize the 3rd person impersonal pronoun. In all instances, the brothers demonstrate a detached relationship to Yosef. Never is the term "brother" used. Only Reuven and Yehudah, the two brothers who attempt to save Yosef, relate to him in a more endearing way. A comparison of their language, however, reveals the differences in their character. Reuven utilizes the term "the boy" הילד when he returns to the pit and finds Yosef gone. Yehudah, on the other hand, refers to Yosef as "our brother" אחינו and "our brother, our flesh" אחינו בשרינו. Reuven relates to Yosef as the older brother who is bound by the hierarchy of the family to take responsibility for the younger brother. He uses the term "child" even though Yosef is already seventeen years old. Yehudah, in contrast, demonstrates that his bond to Yosef is one of brotherhood, an emotional bond. These differences between Reuven and Yehudah are present throughout the ongoing story, and it is, in the final analysis, Yehudah's sense of responsibility toward Binyamin that touches Yosef and leads him to reveal his identity to his brothers.

3. The discussion between God and Moshe at the beginning of the story of the golden calf (Shemot 32:1–14) provides an interesting example in which the use of the expression "your people" (עמך) by both God and Moshe is laden with meaning. When God informs Moshe of the sin, he uses the term "your people" which implies that Moshe in some way bears responsibility for the problem. According to Rashi, the sin of the golden calf was instigated by the ערב רב, the Egyptians whom Moshe had accepted into the group of his own volition. In Moshe's response, his plea on behalf of Bnai Yisrael, he also uses the term "your people." Here, according to several *Midrashim*, Moshe is urging God to see the Bnai Yisrael as his people, regardless of their actions. Moshe implies that the very fact that God has invested so heavily in their fate creates a bond

that cannot be broken by this one act. Another interpretation actually understands Moshe's comment as a counter indictment of God, implying that He in fact bears responsibility for the resulting sin since He provided the people with gold on their way out of Egypt. In either case, the reference to Bnai Yisrael in the final verse of this section indicates that God accepted Moshe's argument: "And God repented of the evil that He had said He would do to **His people** (עמו)."

C. Biblical Dialogue

Biblical dialogue, unlike dialogue in modern literature, does not usually define the emotions of the participants or describe the nuances in the conversation. Nechama pointed out, however, that in the Torah this is at times accomplished through variant uses of the word ויאמר ("and he said") or its feminine or plural equivalents. This phrase is generally utilized in a dialogue each time there is a change of speakers in the conversation. In most cases, the names of the speakers are identified at the beginning of the dialogue, and not thereafter. Nechama identified three common deviations from this pattern:

1. Identification of the Speaker in the Course of the Dialogue: Sometimes the Torah will utilize the name of the speaker at a later point in the conversation. According to Nechama, this indicates the added significance of that particular point in the dialogue. For example, the dialogue between Yitzchak and Avraham on the way to the akeidah (Bereishit 22:7–8):

ויאמר : "אבי".
ויאמר : "הנני בני".
ויאמר : "הנה האש והעצים ואיה השה לעולה".
ויאמר **אברהם** : "א-להים יראה לו השה לעלה בני".

And he said: "My father."
And he said: "I am here my son."
And he said: "Behold, here are the fire and the wood, but where is the lamb for the offering."
And **Avraham** said: "God will show us the lamb for the offering, my son."

The insertion of Avraham's name at this point reflects the importance and heaviness of the statement. One can imagine the emotional impact that this statement had on Avraham.

2. Identifying the Indirect Object: The Torah will at times include a reference to the person or people who are being spoken to, i.e., ויאמר לו ("and he said to him"). By doing so, the Torah is indicating a greater level of engagement. This is evident in Yaacov' dialogue with the shepherds in his search for the house of Lavan (Bereishit 29:4–6):

ויאמר **להם** יעקב: "אחי מאין אתם?"
ויאמרו: "מחרן אנחנו".
ויאמר **להם**: "הידעתם את לבן בן נחור?"
ויאמרו: "ידענו".
ויאמר **להם**: "השלום לו?"
ויאמרו: "שלום והנה רחל בתו באה עם הצאן".

And Yaacov said **to them**: "My brothers, where are you from?"
And they said: "We are from Harran."
And he said **to them**: "Do you know Lavan the son of Nachor?"
And they said: "We know."
And he said **to them**: "Is he well?"
And they said: "He is well. And behold his daughter Rachel is coming with the sheep."

It is obvious that Yaacov is the initiator and the interested party in this conversation, while the shepherds are quite indifferent.

3. Repetition of ויאמר When There Is No Change of Speaker:

According to Nechama, the use of the word ויאמר when there is no change of speaker represents a "pregnant pause." This pause at times reflects a sense of dismay or confusion on the part of the listener, as in Shemot 3:4–6:

ויקרא אליו א-להים מתוך הסנה

ויאמר : "משה משה".

ויאמר : "הנני".

ויאמר : "אל תקרב הלם של נעליך מעל רגליך כי המקום אשר אתה עומד עליו אדמת קדש הוא".

ויאמר : "אנכי א-להי אביך..."

And God called to him [Moshe] from the bush
And He said: "Moshe, Moshe."
And he said: "I am here."
And He said: "Do not come near. Take your shoes off of your feet for the place upon which you stand is holy ground."
And He said: "I am the God of your fathers …"

In this case, the pause gives Moshe time to take off his shoes, but also to internalize the awesome message that he has received.

This pause can also reflect the anticipation of the listener. This is reflected in Tzidkiyahu's conversation with Yirmiyahu in Yirmiyahu 37:17. The fearful Tzidkiyahu had summoned the prophet to see if he had received a prophecy regarding his fortunes:

ויאמר : "היש דבר מאת ה'?"
ויאמר ירמיהו : "יש".
ויאמר : "ביד מלך בבל תנתן".

And he said: "Is there any word from the Lord?"
And Yirmiyahu said: "There is."
And he said: "You shall be delivered into the hand of the
King of Bavel."

This literary device subtly gives the reader the sense of fear and
anticipation felt by Tzidkiyahu during this brief pause that must
have seemed to him like an eternity.

The pause reflected in the repetition of ויאמר can also indicate the
lack of an anticipated reaction, the negotiations between Moshe
and the tribes of Reuven and Gad in Bamidbar 32:2–5:

ויאמרו אל משה ואל אלעזר הכהן ואל נשיאי העדה לאמר :
...הארץ אשר הכה ה' לפני עדת ישראל ארץ מקנה הוא לעבדיך
מקנה".
ויאמרו: "אם מצאנו חן בעיניך יתן את הארץ הזאת
לעבדיך לאחזה אל תעברנו את הירדן".

And they said to Moshe and to Elazar the Priest and to
the Princes of the Congregation saying: ...The land that the
Lord smote before the Congregation of Israel is a land for
cattle, and your servants have cattle."
And they said: "If we have found favor in your eyes,
let this land be given to your servants as a possession, and
bring us not over the Jordan.

In this case the representatives of the tribes of Reuven and Gad
hoped that Moshe would react to their introduction and suggest on
his own that they remain in the grazing land on the other side of

the Jordan. After an uncomfortable silence, they proceed with their presentation and make the suggestion themselves.

D. Association: סמיכות

The concept of סמיכות פרשיות is commonly used by Midrash Halacha and some classical commentators to explain the juxtaposition of certain laws in the Biblical text. While the flow of the narrative sections of the Torah is usually understandable, the structure of the legal sections often begs for explanation. סמיכות פרשיות assumes that the laws in the Torah are not randomly placed. Ibn Ezra states in his commentary to Parshat Mishpatim (21:2) that although each law stands on its own, there is a reason for the placement of all of the laws in the Torah: "If we are unable [to understand the reason], we must consider it a lack in our knowledge." Thus, the attempt to understand the reason for the juxtaposition of certain laws can uncover additional layers of meaning.

Most students of Chumash and Rashi are familiar with סמיכות as it relates to the connection between two sections of the Torah. For example:

למה נסמכה פרשת נזיר לפרשת סוטה? לומר לך שכל הרואה סוטה בקלקולה יזיר עצמו מן היין שהוא מביא לידי ניאוף. (רש"י, במדבר ו, ב)

Why is the section dealing with the Nazir connected to the section dealing with the Sotah? To teach you that one who sees a sotah in her disgrace will vow not to drink wine, for it leads to adultery. (Rashi, Bamidbar 6:2)

Nechama demonstrated, however, that סמיכות applies as well to laws within one section, and even within one verse. The classic question, "Why is this law connected to that law?" can be asked of students in order to foster an analysis of the structure and meaning of the legal portions of the text. This question is somewhat open ended, and allows for the subjective opinion of the student. Ideas can be checked against the opinions of the commentators.

Generally, the juxtaposition of laws achieves one of two purposes according to the Midrash:

1. **Causality:** Based on the Mishnaic dictum, "The performance of a mitzvah brings in its wake another mitzvah, and the performance of a transgression brings in its wake another transgression" (Avot 4:2), the commentators find causality to be the reason for the juxtaposition of some laws. A classical example of this approach is Chapter 25 in Vayikra that includes a variety of laws:

25:1–13:	laws of shemittah and yovel
25:14–18:	laws relating to the sale of goods
25:19–29:	laws relating to sale of family land
25:29–34:	laws relating to sale of houses
25:35–38:	laws relating to help for the poor including the prohibition of lending with interest
25:39–46:	laws relating to slaves
25:47–55:	laws relating to one who sells himself to a non-Jew

Rashi views the structure of the section as a warning against the progressive results of avarice:

רש״י (כו:א) : ואף הפרשיות הללו נאמרו על הסדר. בתחילה
הזהיר על השביעית, ואם חמד ממון ונחשד על השביעית סופו
למכור מטלטליו, לכך סמך לה : וכי תמכרו ממכר... לא חזר בו,
סוף מוכר אחוזתו, לא חזר בו, סוף מוכר את ביתו, לא חזר בו,
סוף לווה בריבית... לא חזר בו, סוף מוכר את עצמו, לא חזר בו,
לא דיו לישראל אלא אפילו לגוי.

111

Rashi (26:1): Indeed all of these sections are listed in the sequence in which the incidents to which they refer actually occur. First the Torah warns about the sabbatical year produce [not to trade]. If, however, one is covetous of money and brings himself under the suspicion of trading in produce of the seventh year, he will at some time have to sell his movable property out of destitution. It is for this reason that the Torah puts in juxtaposition to it the section dealing with the selling of movable property.... If he does not desist from it, he will be afterwards forced to sell his landed property; if he still does not leave off, as time goes on he will have to sell his house. If he does still not give it up, he will have to borrow money on interest.... If he still does not mend his ways, as time goes on he will be compelled to sell himself as a slave to another Jew. If after his release he still does not abandon his evil ways, it will not be enough punishment for him that he has once sold himself to a Jew, but he will then be compelled to sell himself again even to a heathen.

2. **Limitation:** In some cases, the commentators explain that the juxtaposition of two laws is intended to have one law place limits on the other – i.e., this law is applicable in all cases except this one. The following section from Devarim 22:9–12 is an example:

ט. לא תזרע כרמך כלאים....

י. לא תחרש בשור ובחמור יחדו

יא. לא תלבש שעטנז צמר ופשתים יחדו

יב. גדלים תעשה לך על ארבע כנפות כסותך אשר תכסה בה.

9) You shall not sow your vineyard with diverse seeds....

10) You shall not plow with an ox and an ass together.

11) You shall not wear a garment of diverse kinds, of wool and linen together.

12) You shall make fringes on the four corners of your garment with which you cover yourself.

In this case, students might first be asked to notice the apparent distinction between the last verse and the previous three. Verses 9-11 all deal with prohibited mixtures, while verse 12 does not. The Midrash explains that this fourth verse comes to limit the previous law – i.e., although it is generally prohibited to have clothing that combines wool and linen, this mixture is permitted in the case of tzitzit.

Rashi utilizes both approaches in the two explanations that he suggests to explain the connection between Devarim 19:16-21 and Devarim 20:1-9. The end of chapter 19 deals with the issue of false testimony, with the final verse describing the punishment of the witnesses as "an eye for an eye, a tooth for a tooth, a foot for a foot." The beginning of chapter 20 deals with the laws of warfare:

רש"י כ, א: כי תצא למלחמה: סמך הכתוב יציאת מלחמה לכאן, לומר לך שאין מחוסר אבר יוצא למלחמה. דבר אחר: לומר לך אם עשית משפט צדק מובטח אתה שאם תצא למלחמה אתה נוצח.

> **Rashi** 20:1: When you go out to war: The Torah placed laws relating to going out to war here in proximity to teach that one who is lacking a limb does not go to war. Another explanation: To teach you that if you implement righteous judgement, you are assured that if you go out to war you will triumph.

Students might be asked to speculate on the connection between the two sections, and then to compare the two answers of Rashi.

Rashi's first explanation is one of limitation, that one who is maimed does not have the obligation to go to war. The second explanation is one of causality, that the fostering of justice will lead to victory in war.

E. Parallelism

Parallelism is a standard poetic form in Biblical poetry in which seemingly equivalent expressions are used consecutively. Commentators differ with regard to the significance that they attribute to the repetitions in parallelism. Ibn Ezra, consistent with his position on recapitulation and extraneous language, feels that parallelism is simply a literary convention without exegetical meaning. Rashi is inconsistent with regard to parallelism, at times interpreting the repetitive phrases and at times not. The Malbim believes that parallelism is intended to express two ideas, and he, therefore, consistently interprets sections that exhibit this style.

The following is an example of the Malbim's interpretation on Yaacov's blessing of Shimon and Levi (Bereshit 49:5–7):

שמעון ולוי אחים כלי חמס מכרותיהם"
בסדם אל תבוא נפשי
בקהלם אל תחד כבדי
כי באפם הרגו איש
וברצונם עקרו שור
ארור אפם כי עז
ועברתם כי קשתה"....

"Shimon and Levi are brothers, instruments of cruelty are their swords.
In their covert council let my soul not come,
In their assembly let my honor not be united.
For in their anger they killed a man,
And by their will they uprooted an ox.

114

Cursed be their anger for it is strong,

And their fury, for it is hard...."

The section includes several examples of parallelism as indicated by the bold and italicized sections. The Malbim interprets each as follows:

1. "בסודם..." – לא היה על פי עצתי ואני לא ידעתי מזה".
"ובקהלם..." – ואחר כך בקהלם כשנקהלו ויבאו על העיר".

2. "באפם הרגו איש..." – מה שהרגו אנשי שכם היה מתוך אף וכעס לא לשם ה' או להציל כבודי.
"ברצונם עקרו שור..."-אחר שנחה חמתם... לקחו בשלל מקניהם ועקרו את השורים".

3. "ארור אפם..." – כי הוא עז יותר מן המדה. ויש הבדל בין אף ובין עברה, שאף היא מה שקוצף על מי שחטא כנגדו.
"ועברתם כי קשתה..." – ישולח חרונו גם על מי שלא חטא...ונגד אנשי שכם היה עברה.

1. In their covert council…" – I was not involved in the initial stages of the planning of the attack.

"In their assembly…" – I was also not involved when they banded together and descended on the city.

2. "In their anger they killed a man…" – Their massacre of the men of Shechem was perpetrated in anger, not for the sake of God or my honor.

"And by their will they uprooted an ox…" – Even after their anger subsided, they continued their cruelty by taking the animals.

3. "Cursed be their anger (אפם), for it is strong," The Malbim distinguishes between anger (אף), which is directed at one who has caused harm, and fury (עברה) that spills over to those who have done no wrong. Thus, this phrase refers to their anger that was directed against Shechem ben Chamor, who had violated their sister.

"and their fury, for it is hard." – This refers to the fury that overflowed and led them to kill the men of Shechem who had not done anything wrong.

The Malbim's distinction between different expressions of anger appears again in his interpretation of another example of parallelism that is found in a familiar section of Tehillim (78:38):

"והוא רחום יכפר עוון ולא ישחית **והרבה להשיב אפו** ולא יעיר
כל חמתו"

"And he was full of compassion, forgiving iniquity, and he did not destroy them, often **he returned his anger** *and did not stir up his wrath.*"

In this case, again, the Malbim differentiates between anger (אף) and wrath (חמה). As indicated before, anger refers to the immediate reaction that is directed at one who has done harm. Wrath is an anger that one keeps inside and continues to smolder until it explodes outward. Thus, according to the Malbim, the psalmist praises God for returning the anger that had already been expressed, and for preventing the smoldering wrath from coming to expression.

CHAPTER VIII

MODEL LESSON I: A LEGAL SECTION
VAYIKRA 19:1–18 – קדושים תהיו

Chapters eight and nine provide model lessons that are designed to demonstrate how the various components of Nechama's methodology can be combined to create educationally effective units of study. This chapter demonstrates the use of the methodology in teaching a legal section of the Torah, and chapter 9 demonstrates its application to teaching a narrative section.

א. וידבר ה׳ אל משה לאמור:

ב. דבר אל כל עדת בני ישראל ואמרת אליהם קדשים תהיו כי קדוש אני ה׳ א-להיכם.

ג. איש אמו ואביו תיראו ואת שבתתי תשמרו אני ה׳ א-להיכם.

ד. אל תפנו אל האלילם ואלהי מסכה לא תעשו לכם אני ה׳ א-להיכם.

ה. וכי תזבחו זבח שלמים לה׳ לרצנכם תזבחהו.

ו. ביום זבחכם יאכל וממחרת והנותר עד יום השלישי באש ישרף.

ח. ואם האכל יאכל ביום השלישי פגול הוא לא ירצה.

ט. ואכליו עונו ישא כי את קדש ה׳ חלל ונכרתה הנפש ההיא מעמיה.

י. ובקצרכם את קציר ארצכם לא תכלה פאת שדך לקצר ולקט קצירך לא תלקט.

יא. וכרמך לא תעולל ופרט כרמך לא תלקט לעני ולגר תעזב אתם אני ה׳ א-להיכם.

יב. לא תגנבו ולא תכחשו ולא תשקרו איש בעמיתו.

יג. ולא תשבעו בשמי לשקר וחללת את שם א-להיך אני ה'.

יד. לא תעשוק את רעך ולא תגזול לא תלין פעולת שכיר אתך עד בקר.

טו. לא תקלל חרש ולפני עור לא תתן מכשול ויראת מא-להיך אני ה'.

טז. לא תעשו עול במשפט לא תשא פני דל ולא תהדר פני גדול בצדק תשפט עמיתך.

יז. לא תלך רכיל בעמיך לא תעמד על דם רעך אני ה'.

יח. לא תשנא את אחיך בלבבך הוכח תוכיח את עמיתך ולא תשא עליו חטא.

יט. לא תקם ולא תטר את בני עמך ואהבת לרעך כמוך אני ה'.

1) And the Lord spoke to Moshe saying:

2) Speak to all of the congregation of Israel, and say to them: You shall be holy, for I the Lord your God am holy.

3) You shall fear every man his mother and father, and keep my sabbaths, I am the Lord your God.

4) Turn not to idols, nor make for yourselves molten gods; I am the Lord your God.

5) And if you offer a sacrifice of a peace offering to God, you shall offer it so that it be favorably accepted.

6) It shall be eaten on the same day you offer it and on the following day, and if anything remain on the third day, it shall be burned in fire.

7) And if it be eaten on the third day, it is an abomination and shall not be accepted.

8) One who eats it shall bear his iniquity, for he has profaned the hallowed thing of God, and that soul shall be cut off from among his people.

9) And when you reap the harvest of your land, you shall not completely reap the corner of your field, nor shall you gather the gleaning of your harvest.

10) And you shall not glean your vineyard, nor shall you gather the single grapes of your vineyard, but you shall leave them for the poor and the stranger, I am the Lord your God.

11) You shall not steal, nor deal falsely, nor lie to one another.

12) And you shall not swear by my name falsely, nor shall you profane the name of your God, I am the Lord.

13) You shall not defraud your neighbor, nor rob him, and you shall not keep over the wages of a hired worker until the morning.

14) You shall not curse the deaf, nor put a stumbling block before the blind, and you shall fear your God.

15) You shall not do unrighteousness in judgement; you shall not raise up the poor nor honor the great, but in righteousness you shall judge your neighbor.

16) You shall not go as a talebearer among your people, nor shall you stand idly by the blood of your neighbor, I am the Lord.

17) You shall not hate your brother in your heart; you shall surely rebuke your neighbor and not suffer sin on his account.

18) You shall not avenge nor bear any grudge against the children of your people, but you shall love your neighbor as yourself, I am the Lord.

Introductory Activity

A. This section is appropriate for Nechama's technique of dividing the text into several parts. Students might be asked to divide the laws in this section into three categories. The following are some of the possibilities that might arise:

1. a. Laws between man and God.
    b. Laws between man and man.
    c. Laws that are both.

2. a. Laws that relate to thought.
b. Laws that relate to speech
c. Law that relate to action.

3. a. Laws ending with the statement "I am the Lord" or "I am the Lord your God."
b. Laws ending with the phrase "And you shall fear your God."
c. Laws with no such ending.

No matter what categories the students create, the activity requires them to preview all of the laws in this section and to pay attention to nuances that distinguish them. The first two examples, would require that the students consider where the statement "you shall be holy" fits in. This is an issue that the teacher can deal with in a subsequent lesson.

B. An alternative introductory lesson relates to a Midrash in Vayikra Rabbah 24:5 which states that Parshat Kedoshim contains within it references to all of the ten commandments. Nine of the references appear in our section. Students might be shown the reference to the prohibition of adultery in verse 20:10, and then be asked to find the nine other references in our section. Some of the references are clear, others require discernment and can generate discussion. The following are the determinations of the Midrash:

1. "I am the Lord your God" – 19:2
2. "Do not have any other gods" – 19:4
3. "Do not take the name of God in vain" – 19:12
4. "Remember the Shabbat" – 19:3
5. "Honor your father and mother" – 19:3
6. "Do not murder" – 19:16 ("Do not stand idly by the blood…")
7. "Do not steal" – 19:11

8. "Do not bear false witness" – 19:16 ("Do not go tale-bearing")
9. "Do not covet" – 19:18 ("Love your neighbor as yourself")

Besides fostering a review of the ten commandments, this exercise forces students to preview and give thought to the laws in this section.

Choosing Focal Points

The 18 verses reproduced in this section present a vast amount of potential material for instruction. Nechama dedicated almost 100 pages of her *Iyunim Hadashim beSefer Vayikra*, over 20% of the entire book, to this section. Obviously, one could spend months studying the beginning of Parshat Kedoshim. Nechama's belief in maintaining a reasonable pace in the teaching of Torah to students in elementary and high school, however, requires the selection of several particular points of focus.

As was stated previously, along with the pedagogical goals relating to the technical aspects of textual analysis and parshanut, it was very important to Nechama that the lessons have an educational message. In this model instructional unit, the message of each component is part of a larger whole. The larger concept is found in the interpretation of the Ramban in the first unit (verse 2). The Ramban makes a distinction between law and morality, positing that the Torah requires us to aspire to a level of holiness that is not defined merely by adherence to legal proscriptions. In other words, while the law can serve as a general guideline for our behavior, it can not ensure moral conduct. Each of the units selected for this section relates in some way to this general theme, as will be specified at the conclusion of this chapter.

The following is an example of a model unit based on this Torah section:

A. 19:2 - "קדושים תהיו" – "You shall be holy"

רש"י: הוו פרושים מן העריות ומן העבירה, שכל מקום שאתה מוצא גדר ערוה אתה מוצא קדושה.

Rashi: Be separate from promiscuity and from sin, for every place where you find prohibited categories of promiscuity, you find the concept of holiness.

רמב"ן: והענין כי התורה הזהירה בעריות ובמאכלים האסורים והתירה הביאה איש באשתו ואכילת הבשר והיין, א"כ ימצא בעל התאוה מקום להיות שטוף בזימת אשתו או נשיו הרבות, ולהיות בסובאי יין בזוללי בשר למו... והנה יהיה נבל ברשות התורה, לפיכך בא הכתוב אחרי שפרט האיסורים שאסר אותם לגמרי, וצוה בדבר כללי שנהיה פרושים מן המותרות.

Ramban: And the point is that that the Torah prohibited promiscuity and prohibited foods, and permitted sexual relations between a man and his wife and the eating of meat and wine. As such, a person of appetite will find room to be "promiscuous" with his wife or his many wives, and to be a drunkard and a glutton... and he will be a disgusting person within the permit of the Torah. Therefore, after the Torah came and specified those things that are completely forbidden, it commanded in a general sense that we should separate ourselves from those things that are permitted.

Questions:

1. What is the difficulty that both commentators are trying to solve?

2. Do Rashi and Ramban agree or differ on the meaning of the term "קדושים"?

3. According to which commentator is this verse a conclusion to the previous section, and according to which is it an introduction to the subsequent section?

4. What is the difference between the views of Rashi and Ramban regarding the legal significance of this verse?

Suggested Answers:

1. The difficulty: If the Torah gave us 613 commandments, what is the need for a directive to be holy? Presumably, if we follow all of the commandments, we will be holy.

2. Both commentators translate "קדושים" as "פרושים", "separate". According to Rashi, it is a directive to separate oneself from promiscuity, and according to Ramban, it is a directive to separate oneself from things that are permitted.

3. According to Rashi, the verse is a conclusion to the final section of Parshat Acharei Mot that deals with prohibited relationships. According to Ramban, it is an introduction to the laws in Parshat Kedoshim.

4. According to Rashi, this statement is not an additional law, but rather a special warning relating to a particularly important set of prohibitions. Ramban sees it as an additional requirement governing areas not covered in the 613 mitzvot.

B. 19:3 – As indicated earlier, this verse allows for a comparison with the mitzvah of honoring parents that appears in the ten commandments. For a discussion of that comparison, see Chapter 3, Section 2. This verse also allows for a discussion of סמיכות, the juxtaposition of two seemingly unrelated laws in one verse. It is interesting to note that a similar juxtaposition occurs in the ten commandments.

רש"י: ואת שבתתי תשמרו: סמך שבת למורא אב, לומר אף על פי שהזהרתיך על מורא אב, אם יאמר לך: חלל את השבת, אל תשמע לו, וכן בשאר כל המצוות.
אני ה' א-להיכם: אתה ואביך חייבים בכבודי, לפיכך לא תשמע לו לבטל את דברי.

Rashi: Observe My Shabbatot: It connects the observance of shabbat to the fear of parents to say that even though I warned you regarding fear of parents, you should not listen to them if they tell you to desecrate shabbat or other *mitzvot*.

I am the Lord your God: You and your father are required to honor me. Therefore do not listen to him to negate my words.

משך חכמה: דזה אינו מצוייר בשכל, שמצווה שבין אדם לחברו ידחה איסור דברי תורה... רק משום שבכיבוד אביו ואמו יש מה שנוגע לבין אדם למקום... ומסרוה דור אחר דור לזרעם אחריהם, והודיעו בנים לבני בניהם יום אשר עמדו בחורב... ואם דור יבזה אביו ואמו וילעג למוסרי הקבלה, אז תיפסק תורה מישראל...
לכן אפשר להעלות את הדעת שידחה כיבוד אב ואם את השבת.

Meshech Chochmah: It is not logical that a mitzvah between man and man would override a mitzvah between man and God....It is only because honoring parents touches on the relationship between man and God.... They passed it [the tradition], generation after generation, to their children, and children informed their grandchildren of the day that they stood at Sinai.... And if one generation will scorn mothers and fathers and will mock the transmitters of the tradition, Torah will disappear from Israel.... Therefore, it is possible to think that honoring parents would supercede shabbat.

Questions:

1. To what difficulty in Rashi's comment is the Meshech Chochmah relating?

2. How does the Meshech Chochmah resolve the difficulty. How does Rashi's understanding of "I am the Lord your God" support this solution?

Suggested Answers:

1. Rashi's comment is based on an assumption that seems illogical. In Shemot 35, the Torah juxtaposed the mitzvot of shabbat and the building of the mishkan to indicate that God's commandment to build the mishkan does not override shabbat. Certainly, it would seem, a directive by one's parent should not override shabbat. Furthermore, a mitzvah between man and God should take precedence when in conflict with a mitzvah between man and man. And even in strict halachic terms, a positive commandment (honoring parents) would not supercede a positive and negative commandment (shabbat).

2. The Meshech Chochmah explains that because parents are fundamental to passing on the tradition, disrespect of parents could threaten the whole system. We might, therefore, think that respecting parents takes precedence over other mitzvot. According to Rashi, the conclusion of the verse refutes this possibility, for the transmission of the tradition through the parents is based on their subordination to God's will. To respect them when they are negating God's will would be more damaging to the system.

C. 19:9-11 – These verses reflect two issues of סמיכות: 1) Why is the prohibition of stealing connected to the agricultural laws preceding it?, and 2) What is the relationship between the series of laws in verse 11?

אבן עזרא: וטעם "לא תגנבו", אחר כך, כי כן ציויתך שתתן משלך אל העניים לכבוד ה', אף שתקח מה שהוא לאחרים.

Ibn Ezra: The reason that "you shall not steal" is learned afterward [after the law of pe'ah], that as I commanded you to give of yours to the poor in honor of God, so you should not take from what belongs to others.

אור החיים: סמך מצוות גנבה למצוות פאת שדה, אולי שנתכוון על דרך מה שאמרו בתורת כהנים קדושים (כג): בן בג בג אומר: לא תגנוב את שלך מהגנב, שלא תיראה כגנב". וכאן נתכוון במה שסמך "לא תגנבו" לפאה, שבא עליה באזהרה לבל יגנוב אותה, בחושבו כי שלו הוא לוקח.

Ohr Hachaim: The fact that it connected the prohibition of stealing to the mitzvah of pe'ah is perhaps to refer to what was said in the name of the son of Bag Bag: "Do not steal your property from a thief so you don't look like a thief." The connection of "do not steal" to pe'ah comes as a warning that one should not steal from it thinking that it is his.

תולדות יצחק: לפי שמי שאינו מניח פאת שדה הוא כמו גוזל לעני, כמו שאמרו חז"ל (משלי כב, כב): אל תגזול דל כי דל הוא", וכי מה יגזלו מן העני שאין לו? והשיבו: מתנות עניים. מי שלא נתנם להם, גוזל אותם, לכן סמך לזה: "לא תגנבו". ואחשוב עוד: מה שסמך "לא תגנבו" ל "לא תכלה פאת שדך", לפי שמי שאינו נותן צדקה לעני הוא סיבה שיגנוב.

Toldot Yitzchak: One who does not leave a corner of the field is like one who steals from the poor, as it says in Proverbs (22:22), "Do not steal from the poor because he is poor." What can he steal from a poor person that has nothing? The gifts for the poor. One who does not give them, steals them. Another thought: Why is the prohibition of stealing next to the law of pe'ah? One who doesn't give tzedakah to the poor causes him to steal.

Questions:

1. In the interpretations of Ibn Ezra and Ohr Hachaim, one of the two laws is extrapolated from the other. Which law informs the other in each interpretation?

2. Toldot Yitzchak provides two possible explanations for the juxtaposition of the two laws. Do they correspond to the explanations of Ibn Ezra and Ohr Hachaim, or does he add something new?

3. How does the verse from Proverbs support Toldot Yitzchak's first explanation?

4. Why in their explanations do the commentators discuss the connection between the prohibition to steal and the law of pe'ah rather than to the other agricultural laws that directly precede it?

Suggested Answers:

1. According to Ibn Ezra, the prohibition of stealing flows from the law of pe'ah (a קל וחומר argument). According to Ohr Hachaim, the law of stealing adds another dimension to the law of pe'ah (that you must take extra care not to utilize the pe'ah yourself).

2. The first explanation of Toldot Yitzchak is similar to that of Ohr Hachaim in that the law of pe'ah is illuminated by the prohibition of stealing. He, however, extends the principle – that one who refrains from giving any obligatory gift to the poor is considered a thief. The second explanation is completely different from those of Ibn Ezra and Ohr Hachaim.

3. The verse from proverbs discusses stealing from the poor. The only way it would be possible to steal from a person who is extremely poor would be to withhold tzedakah from him.

4. The law of pe'ah differs from the other laws mentioned in the two verses. The others relate to things which are forgotten or not worth harvesting. In pe'ah the owner of the field actively puts aside desirable produce that he would be pleased to use for himself. It is, therefore, a more appropriate example for these explanations.

רש"י:(יט, יא)– אם גנבת סופך לכחש, סופך לשקר, סופך לישבע
לשקר.

Rashi: (19:11) – If you steal, you will inevitably deal falsely, you will inevitably lie, and you will inevitably swear falsely [found at the beginning of verse 12].

Questions:

1. What is the difference between the reason that Rashi gives for the juxtaposition of the laws in verses 12–13 and the reason that he gives for the juxtaposition of the laws in verse 3?

2. Do the two explanations of Toldot Yitzchak for the juxtaposition of the law of pe'ah and the prohibition of stealing correspond to the models found in Rashi, or do they have a different purpose?

Suggested Answers:

1. In this case, the juxtaposition reflects a causality between the several mitzvot in the verses. In verse 3, one law comes to limit the jurisdiction of the other.

2. The second explanation in Toldot Yitzchak reflects a causality between the two laws, similar to Rashi's explanation here. His first explanation, however, has a different function - the second law comes to explain and emphasize the significance of the first.

D. 19: 13-14 – Verse 13 allows for comparison with the same law that appears in Devarim 24: 14-15, and verse 14 allows for a comparison with four other instances in which the same ending phrase is utilized:

Definitions of עושק:

בבא מציעא קיא, ע"א: איזה הוא עושק ואיזהו גזל? לך ושוב,
לך ושוב – זה הוא עושק: יש בידי ואיני נותן לך – זה הוא גזל.

Baba Metzia 111a: What is עושק and what is גזל? Go and come back, go and come back – this is עושק; I have it and won't give it to you – this is גזל.

רמב"ם: (הלכות גזילה ואבידה א, ג–ד) איזהו גוזל? זה הלוקח
ממון האדם בחזקה... איזהו עושק? זה שבא ממון חברו לתוך
ידו ברצון הבעלים, וכיון שתבעוהו, כבש הממון אצלו בחזקה
ולא החזירו.

Rambam (הלכות גזילה ואבידה א, ג–ד): What is גזל? One who takes another's property by force…. What is עושק? One who receives the property of another with the consent of the owner, and when he comes to claim it, he retains it by force.

רש"י: "לא תעשוק" זה הכובש שכר שכיר.

Rashi: לא תעשק: This refers to retaining the wages of a worker.

Comparison to Devarim 24:14–15:

יד) לא תעשק שכיר עני ואביון מאחיך או מגרך אשר בארצך
בשעריך.
טו) ביומו תתן שכרו ולא תבוא עליו השמש כי עני הוא ואליו
הוא נשא את נפשו...

14) You shall not defraud a hired worker that is poor or
needy, whether he be of your brethren or of the strangers
that are in your land in your gates.
15) You shall give him his wages on his day, and the sun
shall not set on it, for he is poor and sets his heart on it....

רש"י: (דברים כד, יד) לא תעשק שכיר, והלא כבר כתוב, אלא
לעבור על האביון בשני לאווין: לא תעשק שכר שכיר שהוא עני
ואביון, ועל העשיר כבר הוזהר. (ויקרא יט, יג)

Rashi: (Devarim 24:14) לא תעשק שכיר: Wasn't it already
written? But [it teaches] that with a poor person, one transgresses two prohibitions: you shall not withhold the wages
of a worker who is poor and needy; and with regard to a
wealthy person, there was already a warning [in Vayikra
19:13].

רש"י: ויקרא יט, יג: "עד בקר": בשכיר יום הכתוב מדבר
שיציאתו משתשקעה החמה, לפיכך זמן גבוי שכרו כל הלילה,
ובמקום אחר הוא אומר: "ולא תבא עליו השמש" מדבר בשכיר
לילה שהשלמת פעולתו משיעלה עמוד השחר, לפיכך זמן גבוי
שכרו כל היום, לפי שנתנה תורה זמן לבעל הבית עונה לבקש
מעות.

Rashi: (Vayikra 19:13) עד בקר: The verse is talking about a
day worker who finishes at sundown, so that the time for
collecting his wages is all night; and in another place it says

130

"the sun shall not set on it," talking about a night worker who completes his job at sunrise, so that the time for the collection of his wages is all day. For the Torah gave the employer time to prepare the money.

רמב"ן: דברים כד, טו: וטעם "ביומו תתן שכרו" על דרך הפשט, באור ממה שנאמר בתורה (ויקרא יט יג) "לא תלין פעולת שכיר אתך עד בקר"...והמנהג לשכור הפועל ביום אחד ולערב הוא יוצא טרם בוא השמש, ויצווה הכתוב לפרעה ביומו, בהשלים מלאכתו מיד, ושלא תבוא עליו השמש.

Ramban: The simple meaning is that it explains what was said in the Torah (Vayikra 19:13) "you shall not keep over the wages of a hired worker until morning...." It is customary to hire a worker for the day, and in the evening he leaves before sundown. And the verse commands that you pay him on that day immediately as he completes his work, and that the sun should not set on it.

Questions:

1. What is the difference between לא תעשק and לא תלין according to Rashi?

2. What are the differences between the law as recorded in Vayikra and in Devarim?

3. What is the difference between Rashi and Ramban regarding the purpose for recording the law in Devarim?

4. Who is more demanding on the employer, Rashi or Ramban?

Suggested Answers:

1. לא תעשק *refers to withholding wages, and* לא תלין *refers to delaying payment.*

2. *There are two main differences:*
    *a. Vayikra refers to "your neighbor" (*רעך*), and Devarim refers to "the worker who is poor and needy."*
    *b. The time for payment in Vayikra is "until the morning" (*עד בוקר*) and in Devarim it is "until sunset" (*לא תבוא עליו השמש*).*

3. *According to Rashi, the law in Devarim adds new legislation: a) It adds an additional prohibition for withholding the wages of needy workers, and b) It gives the law for a night laborer as opposed to the law for a day worker recorded in Vayikra. According to Ramban, the law as recorded in Devarim does not add new legislation, but further explains the law in Vayikra regarding the required time of payment.*

4. *The Ramban is more demanding on the employer, requiring immediate payment at the end of the work day. Rashi allows the employer up to 12 hours from the conclusion of the job to pay the workers.*

Verse 19:14:

ספרא: לא תקלל חרש: אין לי אלא חרש, מניין לרבות כל אדם?
תלמוד לומר (שמות כב, כז) : "ונשיא בעמך לא תאור".

Sifre: You shall not curse the deaf: This only refers to the deaf. How do I know that it includes all people? The Torah teaches us (Shemot 22:27) "A prince among your people, you shall not curse (נשיא בעמך לא תאור)."

רש"י: אין לי אלא חרש, מנין לרבות כל אדם? תלמוד לומר:
"בעמך לא תאור". (שמות כב, כז)

Rashi: This only refers to the deaf. How do I know that it includes all people? The Torah teaches us (Shemot 22:27) "Among your people you shall not curse (בעמך לא תאור)."

רמב״ן: [מתייחס לפירושו של רש״י] אבל המדרש בגמרא אינו כן, אלא הזהיר הכתוב בנכבדים בעם, הדיין והנשיא...וחזר והזהיר באומללים שבעם והוא החרש, ומהם ילמדו בנין אב אל כל שאר העם, כי מן הראש ועד הסוף הכל בכלל האזהרה.

Ramban: [referring to Rashi's commentary] But the Midrash in the Gemara (Sanhedrin 66a) is not so, rather it mentions the respected among the people, the judge and the prince...and it returns and mentions the wretched among the people – the deaf. And from them you can learn by deduction regarding all of the people, from top to bottom, all are included in the warning.

רש״י: ולפני עור לא תתן מכשול: הסומא בדבר לא תתן עצה שאינה הוגנת לו.

Rashi: And do not place a stumbling block before the blind: Before one who is blind in a certain matter, do not give him advice that is not appropriate for him.

אלשיך: "לא תלין פעולת שכיר", כי אם כה תעשה, אתה גורם עבירות רבות. האחד כי בלכת הדל לביתו בידים ריקות... והאשה וילדנה תשאנה עיניהן אל ידיו להריק להם... אז יתן את קולו בבכי וקרא ואמר: ארור האיש אשר עשיתי עמו היום מלאכה. על כן עליו (הדל) אני מצווה ואומר "לא תקלל חרש" ועל העשיר הוא אומר "ולפני עור לא תתן מכשל".

Alshich: "You shall not hold over the worker's wage," for if you do so, you will cause many sins. One is that when the poor returns to his house empty handed...and his wife and children will see his empty hands…he will raise his voice in a cry and say, "cursed is the man for whom I worked today." Therefore, to him (the poor man) I command: "Do not curse the deaf" and to rich say "Do not place a stumbling block before the blind."

The following four other verses end with the phrase "and you shall fear your God":

Vayikra 19:32 – respect for the elderly
Vayikra 25:17 – verbal fraud – misleading someone with bad advice
Vayikra 25:36 – prohibition of charging interest
Vayikra 25:43 – prohibition of giving unnecessary work to a slave.

רש״י: וכן כל דבר המסור ללבו של אדם העושהו ואין שאר
הבריות מכירות בו נאמר בו : ויראת מא-להיך.

Rashi: And so everything that is given to the heart of the perpetrator, and others cannot recognize it [either the act or the intent], for that it says "and you shall fear your God [who knows your thoughts]."

Questions:

1. Why does Rashi deviate from the wording of the Midrash in his explanation regarding the cursing of the deaf? Why, according to the Ramban, was it not necessary to change the wording? How might the following verse be used by the Ramban to help support his position: "And it came to pass, that at midnight God smote all of the firstborn in the land of Egypt, from the firstborn of Paroah that sits on his throne to the firstborn of the captive in the dungeon…" (Shemot 12:29)?

2. What is the reason, according to Rashi, for the phrase "and you shall fear your God" in this verse? Explain how it serves the same function in the other four verses in which it is used.

3. How does the phrase "and you shall fear your God" help to explain Rashi's deviation from the simple meaning of "you shall not place a stumbling block before the blind"?

4. Is Alshich's explanation of the juxtaposition of the laws in these verses similar to the model(s) in the explanation of Toldot Yitzchak on verses 19:9-11, or does he offer a new model?

Suggested Answers:

1. The Midrash uses a reference that refers to the upper echelon of society to teach that it is prohibited to curse anybody. Since the lesson is not clear from the context, Rashi emphasizes the word בעמך ("among your people") by not quoting the word נשיא ("prince"). Ramban claims that the emendation is not necessary since the reference to the two extremes of the society is a literary form that is intended to include everyone in the society. This form is demonstrated in the verse in Shemot that defines all of the first born children in the Egyptian society by referring to the son of Paroah and the son of the captive.

2. According to Rashi, the phrase "and you shall fear your God" is utilized when the act cannot be discerned by an observer and can, thus, only be truly known by the perpetrator and by God. In this case, the person being cursed cannot hear it. The following are the reasons for the other four references:

Vayikra 19:32 – respect for the elderly – He can claim that he did not see the elderly person.
Vayikra 25:17 – verbal fraud – misleading someone with bad advice – He can say that he thought that it was good advice and intended no harm.

135

*Vayikra 25:36 – prohibition of charging interest – He might find a
way to legally lend him the money with interest (i.e., through a non-Jew)
and claim that he is benefiting the person.*

*Vayikra 25:43 – prohibition of giving unnecessary work to a slave –
He might claim that from his perspective, the work was necessary.*

*3. Actually placing a stumbling block before a blind person is obvious to
the observer. By defining it as giving bad advice to a person in an area in
which the person receiving the advice lacks expertise, the determination of
wrongdoing becomes less clear. It becomes similar to verbal fraud mentioned in Vayikra 25:17.*

*4. Aspects of Alshich's explanation are actually similar to both of the in-
terpretations of Toldot Yitzchak. The relationship between on-time payment of employees and the prohibition of cursing the deaf is one of causa-
tion, similar to the second explanation in Toldot Yitzchak. The law of
not placing a stumbling block before the blind comes to broaden our understanding of why we must pay workers on time. It is, thus, similar to
the first explanation in Toldot Yitzchak.*

E. 19:17

רמב"ן 1: לא תשנא את אחיך בלבבך: בעבור שדרך השונאים
לכסות את שנאתם בלבם... הוכח תוכח את עמיתך: מצוה
אחרת, ללמדו תוכחת מוסר. ולא תשא עליו חטא: שיהיה עליך
אשם כאשר יחטא ולא הוכחת אותו.

Ramban I: Do not hate your brother in your heart: For it is
the way of those who hate to cover the hatred in their
hearts… you shall surely rebuke your friend: It is a different
mitzvah, to teach you the ethic of rebuke. And not suffer sin
on his account: That you will be blameworthy if he sins and
you had not rebuked him.

רמב"ן 2: והנכון בעיני...אל תשנא את אחיך בלבבך בעשותו לך
שלא כרצונך. אבל, תוכיחנו מדוע ככה עשית עמדי ולא תשא
עליו חטא לכסות שנאתו בלבך ולא תגיד לו. כי בהוכיחך אותו
יתנצל לך, או ישוב ויתודה על חטאו ותכפר לו.

Ramban II: And the correct explanation in my eyes…Do
not hate your brother in your heart when he does something undesirable to you. Rather, rebuke him [by saying]
why did you do this to me, and you will not bear a sin
against him by covering your hatred in your heart and not
telling him. For when you rebuke him, he will apologize to
you or he will confess his sin and achieve atonement.

רש"י: ולא תשא עליו חטא: לא תלבין את פניו ברבים.

Rashi: And do not suffer sin on his account: Do not
embarrass him publicly.

העמק דבר: ולא תשא עליו חטא: כי קרוב שיצדיק עצמו ויוכיח
שלא כמו שמדמה (אתה) או להיפך יבקש מחילה.

Ha'amek Davar: And do not suffer sin on his account:
Because it is probable that he will justify himself and prove
to you that it is not as you imagined, or on the contrary, he
will request forgiveness.

Questions:

1. Why does the Ramban feel that his second explanation is
the correct one? Why does he feel compelled to bring the first
interpretation as well?

2. What is the meaning of the "vav" in ולא תשא עליו חטא
("**and** do not suffer sin on his account") in each explanation?

3. What is the meaning of תשא in each explanation?

4. Whose sin is referred to in the last clause according to each explanation?

Suggested Answers:

1. The second explanation sees the verse in a unified fashion. The hatred is the result of a perceived wrongdoing, and the rebuke is designed to enable him to respond to the perception by clarifying the event or by seeking forgiveness. This explanation also creates a natural connection to the next verse which deals with feelings of revenge. The first explanation sees them as separate unrelated mitzvot. The second commentary is somewhat problematical, however, in that it limits the concept of rebuke to a case in which the individual has been personally wronged. The first interpretation understands the mitzvah of rebuking in a broader sense.

2. *Ramban I* – ו' החיבור – *"and also"*
    Ramban II – ו' התכלית – *"in order that"*
    Rashi – ו' הניגוד – *"but do not"*
    Ha'amek Davar – ו' התכלית – *"in order that"*

3. *Ramban I* – *"do not suffer [a sin]"*
    Ramban II – *"do not bear [a sin against him]" (as in to bear a grudge)*
    Rashi – *"do not commit [a sin]"*
    Ha'amek Davar – *"do not bear [a sin against him]" (as in to bear a grudge)*

4. *Ramban I* – *the rebuker*
    Ramban II – *the one being rebuked*
    Rashi – *the rebuker*
    Ha'amek Davar – *the one being rebuked*

F. 19:18

רש״י : "לא תקם" אמר לו : "השאילני מגלך" אמר לו "לאו".
למחר אמר לו "השאילני קרדומך" אמר לו "איני משאילך כדרך
שלא השאלתני". זו היא נקימה. ואיזו היא נטירה? אמר לו
"השאילני את קרדומך" אמר לו "לאו". למחר אמר לו :
"השאילני מגלך" אמר לו "הא לך, איני כמותך שלא השאלתני",
זו היא נטירה, שנוטר האיבה בלבו אף על פי שאינו נוקם.

Rashi: "You shall not avenge" (נקימה) - He said to him: "Lend me your sickle." He replied: "No." The next day, he said to him: "Lend me your shovel." He replied: "I will not lend it to you, just as you didn't lend me your sickle." Therefore, it says, "You shall not avenge". And what is bearing a grudge? נטירה - He said to him: "Lend me your shovel." And he did not lend it to him. The next day, he said to him: "Lend me your sickle." He replied: "Take it. I'm not like you, that you didn't lend it to me." This is bearing a grudge, that the hatred is retained in the heart even though there is no revenge.

Question:

1. What is the fundamental difference between נקימה and נטירה according to Rashi's definition?

2. In Rashi's example of revenge, he brings the story of the sickle and the shovel. But with regard to bearing a grudge, the order is reversed – shovel first and then sickle. The sickle is a more expensive instrument than a shovel. Try to give a reason for the change in order.

Suggested Answers:

1. נקימה *involves an action, while* נטירה *is in thought only.*

2. In order to differentiate revenge from stinginess, Rashi took an example in which the person was not willing to do even a small favor because the other person had refused to do a larger favor. In נטירה, *even though the person is willing to do a large favor for the person who refused to do him a small favor, he still transgresses if he harbors ill will.*

The concept of "ואהבת לרעך כמוך" ("You shall love your neighbor as yourself") was restated by Hillel in the Gemara (Shabbat 31a) as follows: "That which is hateful to you, do not do to your friend."

The concept also appears in the following section of the Talmud Yerushalmi:

"ואהבת לרעך כמוך"– ר' עקיבא אומר : זה כלל גדול בתורה. בן עזאי אומר : "זה ספר תולדות אדם" (בראשית ה, א) – זה כלל גדול מזה.

"You shall love your neighbor as yourself" - Rabbi Akiva says: This is the great principle of the Torah (כלל גדול בתורה). Ben Azzai says: "This is the book of the generations on man" (Bereishit 5:1) – This is a greater principle than this one.
[Ben Azzai is referring to the following verse: "This is the book of the generations of Man; On the day that God created mankind, in the likeness of God He made him…"]

"זה ספר תולדות אדם ביום ברא א-להים אדם בדמות א-להים עשה אותו".

In the following Gemara (Baba Metzia 62a), Rabbi Akiva seems to qualify his understanding of the concept:

שנים שהיו מהלכין בדרך וביד אחלד מהן קיתון של מים אם
שותין שניהם מתים ואם שותה אחד מהן מגיע לישוב. דרש בן
פטורא מוטב שישתו שניהם וימותו ואל יראה אחד מהם
במיתתו של חבירו. עד שבא ר' עקיבא ולימד "וחי אחיך עמך
חייך קודמים לחיי חבירך".

Two men were walking on the way and in the hands of one
was a flask of water. If they would both drink they would
both die, but if one would drink he would make it to the
settlement. Ben Petura explained: Better that both should
drink and die rather than one seeing the death of his friend.
Until Rabbi Akiva came and taught: "That your brother
shall live with you." (Vayikra 25:36) – your life comes before the life of your friend.

Questions:

1. What are three difficulties with the word כמוך (as yourself)
reflected in these Gemaras?

2. How are they resolved in these texts?

3. Which text is consistent with the following commentary of
the Mendelsohn?[1]

ואין הכתוב מדבר בכמות האהבה, כי אם באיכותה... מצוות ה'
שנאהב את רענו בכל דרכי האהבה אשר בהם נאהב את
עצמינו... ובכל מקום שלא תתנגד אהבת זולתנו לאהבת עצמנו
על צד הצדק, מחוייבים אנו לעשות לזולתתנו כל מה שהיינו
עושים לטובתנו... התורה לא התכוונה כאן אל כמות האהבה כי
אל איכות האהבה.

---

[1] This citation from Mendelsohn appears in his comments on the **Biur** by
Rabbi N.H. Weisel.

The text is concerned with love in its qualitative and not its quantitative sense... God commanded us to love our fellow man just as we love ourselves.... Wherever this love of others does not clash with our own legitimate self interests, we are obliged to promote our fellow man's welfare just as we would our own. The quality must be the same, but not the quantity.

Suggested Answers:

1.   *a. How is it possible in reality to love someone else as much as yourself?*
     b. How can you command someone to love another (an emotion)?
     c. What if you hate yourself? Should you therefore hate others?

2.   *a. Rabbi Akiva's teaching in the Gemara places one's own interests above those of another. Within that context, one must love others. Hillel's formulation also resolves that issue by prohibiting the opposite relationship, which is a more practical injunction.*
     b. Hillel's formulation also resolves this issue by defining the injunction in behavioral terms.
     c. Ben Azzai's statement relates to this issue. He posits that our respect for others must ultimately be based on the fact that man is created in God's image, rather than being related to our own self image.

3.   *Mendelsohn's commentary is consistent with Rabbi Akiva's opinion in the Gemara.*

Note: The controversy between Rabbi Akiva and Ben Azzai could provide material for discussing interesting philosophical points in the classroom. Nechama, however, would advocate utilizing this controversy primarily for the purpose of better understanding the text.

Educational Message

As mentioned earlier, the general theme of this chapter is the relationship between law and morality. Each unit discusses areas requiring moral determinations that are not simply addressed by the legal system, including:

1. the possibility of inappropriate behavior in areas that are permitted, such as eating and drinking;

2. when there is a conflict between the performance of two *mitzvot*, specifically the performance of the same mitzvah for two different people or the performance of two different *mitzvot* (verse 3);

3. the application of the spirit of the law in parallel situations that fall outside of the parameters of the law (verses 9–11);

4. when a particular behavior is not severe, but can lead to more severe behavior on the part of the perpetrator or of the victim;

5. when it may appear that the law should be applied differently to different people (verses 13–14);

6. when the violation of the law is not perceivable and can be interpreted by the perpetrator and others as adherence to the standards of the law (verses 13–14);

7. responsibility for the behavior of others (verse 17);

8. when performance of the law seems to be in conflict with one's own interests, or there is a lack of reciprocity (verse 18).

Thus, this section of Parshat Kedoshim contains not only a wealth of Biblical commentary, but also provides opportunities for the discussion of moral dilemmas that have great relevance to the daily lives of the students. It is incumbent on the teacher to make the connections between the classical texts and situations in the lives of the students that relate to these concepts.

CHAPTER IX

MODEL LESSON II: A NARRATIVE SECTION
בראשית ד' – 16–BEREISHIT 4:1

א. והאדם ידע את חוה אשתו ותהר ותלד את קין ותאמר "קניתי איש את ה'".

ב. ותסף ללדת את אחיו את הבל ויהי הבל רעה צאן וקין היה עבד אדמה.

ג. ויהי מקץ ימים ויבא קין מפרי האדמה מנחה לה'.

ד. והבל הביא גם הוא מבכרות צאנו ומחלבהן וישע ה' אל הבל ואל מנחתו.

ה. ואל קין ואל מנחתו לא שעה ויחר לקין מאד ויפלו פניו.

ו. ויאמר ה' אל קין למה חרה לך ולמה נפלו פניך.

ז. הלוא אם תיטיב שאת ואם לא תיטיב לפתח חטאת רבץ ואליך תשוקתו ואתה תמשול בו.

ח. ויאמר קין אל הבל אחיו ויהי בהיותם בשדה ויקם קין אל הבל אחיו ויהרגהו.

ט. ויאמר ה' אל קין אי הבל אחיך ויאמר לא ידעתי השומר אחי אנכי.

י. ויאמר מה עשית קול דמי אחיך צעקים אלי מן האדמה

יא. ועתה ארור אתה מן האדמה אשר פצתה את פיה לקחת את דמי אחיך מידך.

יב. כי תעבד את האדמה לא תסף תת כחה לך נע ונד תהיה בארץ.

יג. ויאמר קין אל ה' גדול עוני מנשוא.

יד. הן גרשת אתי היום מעל פני האדמה ומפניך אסתר והייתי נע ונד בארץ והיה כל מצאי יהרגני.

טו. ויאמר לו ה׳ לכן כל הרג קין שבעתים יקם וישם ה׳ לקין אות
לבלתי הכות אתו כל מצאו.
טז. ויצא קין מלפני ה׳ וישב בארץ נוד קדמת עדן.

1) And Adam knew Chava his wife, and she conceived and bore Cain saying: "I acquired a man from the Lord."
2) And she bore again, Hevel his brother; And Hevel was a shepherd and Cain was a tiller of the ground.
3) And in the course of time it came to pass that Cain brought from the fruit of the ground an offering to God.
4) And Hevel also brought from the first born of his flocks and of the fat thereof, and God showed favor to Hevel and to his offering.
5) But to Cain and his offering he did not show favor, and Cain was very angry, and his face fell.
6) And God said to Cain: Why are you angry and why are you crestfallen?
7) If you do well, shall you not be accepted? And if you do not do well, sin crouches at the door, and to you shall be its desire. Yet you may rule over him. (based on the Koren translation)
8) And Cain said to Hevel his brother, and it was when they were in the field and Cain rose up against Hevel his brother and killed him.
9) And God said to Cain: Where is Hevel your brother? And he said: I do not know. Am I my brother's keeper?
10) And He said: What have you done? The voice of your brother's blood cries out to me from the ground.
11) And now, cursed are you from the earth, which has opened its mouth to receive your brother's blood from your hand.
12) When you till the ground, it will not continue to give its strength to you. A fugitive and a vagabond shall you be on the earth.

13) And Cain said to God: My sin is too great to bear;

14) Behold you have driven me out this day from the face of the earth, and from your face shall I be hidden; and I shall be a fugitive and a vagabond on the earth, and anyone that finds me will kill me.

15) And God said to him: Therefore, whoever slays Cain, vengeance shall be taken on him sevenfold. And God set a mark on Cain, lest anyone finding him should smite him. (based on the Koren translation)

16) And Cain went out from the presence of the Lord, and dwelt in the land of Nod, to the east of Eden.

Introductory Activity

The narrative in this chapter is quite dramatic in nature. Nechama's introductory techniques involving drama would, therefore, be appropriate. In these activities, students are asked to imagine that they are putting on a play of the story, and are required to answer a question or questions relating to the play. The following are a few possibilities:

1. Changes of Set: Students might be asked to describe the changes of set in the play. This helps them to see the sequence of events in the narrative. The changes of set are as follows:

   a. The births of Cain and Hevel
   b. The offerings of Cain and Hevel
   c. The murder of Hevel
   d. God confronts Cain

2. Title: Students might be asked to give a title for the play. This activity requires them to consider the main focus of the story. The following are some possible responses:

a. The First Murder
b. Sin, Repentance, and Punishment
c. My Brother's Keeper

3. Tone of Dialogue: The teacher can ask the students to find Cain's part in the dialogue. They will discover that Cain is not very talkative. In fact, he only speaks twice, once in verse 9 and once in verses 13-14. In verse 8, the Torah also indicates that a dialogue took place, but the content is not recorded. The students can then be asked to identify the tone of voice in which Cain would deliver his lines – is he defiant? surprised? sarcastic? sad? subdued? This activity requires the students to consider the psychological nuances in the story and can serve as an excellent prelude to some of the commentaries that will be studied on these verses.

Points of Focus

This chapter deals with a number of fundamental issues that are of great relevance to the lives of the students including free will, sin and punishment, repentance, conflict, and sibling rivalry. These issues are discussed in greater detail at the conclusion of this section. In addition, the chapter also includes several paradigms of unique aspects of Rabbinic exegesis.

A. 4:1 – This verse is not essential for an understanding of the main story in this chapter. Nevertheless, it is the first instance of chronological inconsistency, as indicated previously in chapter 6, and is thus worthy of study. In this case, Rashi introduces the grammatical criterion for utilizing this concept:

רש"י: כבר קודם העניין של מעלה קודם שחטא ונטרד מגן עדן, וכן ההריון והלידה, שאם כתב "וידע אדם" נשמע שלאחר שנטרד היו לו בנים.

Rashi: Already before the previous matter, before he sinned and was banished from the Garden of Eden, so to the pregnancy and the birth. For if it had written "and the man knew" ("וידע האדם"), it would imply that after they were banished before they had children. (from Bereishit Rabbah 22:2)

אבן עזרא: כאשר ראה שלא יחיה בגופו בעצמו לעולם הוצרך הוא להחיות המין...

Ibn Ezra: When he realized that he himself would not live forever, he had to give life to the species....

Questions:

1. Translate the beginning of the verse according to Rashi and according to Ibn Ezra.

2. How do Rashi and Ibn Ezra differ with regard to the relationship between the events in chapter 3 and the birth of Cain?

3. What motivates Rashi to interpret the verse as he does? What support might you find for Rashi from the text in previous parts of Bereishit?

Suggested Answers:

1. *Rashi: "And Adam had known Chava..."*
    Ibn Ezra: "And Adam knew Chava..."

2. *According to Rashi, the conception of Cain took place before the sin in the Garden of Eden and was unrelated to it. According to Ibn*

149

Ezra, Adam and Chava only saw the pressing need for procreation after the sin and their resulting mortality.

3. *Rashi is motivated by the use of the imperfect form of the verb וידע האדם as opposed to the regular form of the past tense using the vav hahipukh. He also views procreation as a desirable act unrelated to the sin in the Garden of Eden. Rashi's view is supported by the fact that procreation is commanded in 1:28, well before the sin.*

B. 4:3-4 –

רש״י: מפרי האדמה: מן הגרוע.

Rashi: From the fruit of the ground: From the inferior.

Question:

1. How does Rashi deduce that Cain brought his offering from the inferior produce?

Suggested Answer:

1. *The verse lacks parallelism. It specifies that Hevel brought from the first born animals and from the fat sheep, but does not specify the quality of Cain's offering. This indicates that he specifically refrained from bringing his better quality produce.*

C. 4:6–7

רד״ק: אם תיטיב לבך ומעשיך יהיה לך שאת, ופירוש כפרה וסליחה כמו נושא עון.

Radak: If you improve your heart and your actions, you will have שאת, meaning atonement and forgiveness as in נושא עון.

אבן עזרא: שאת פנים, כי כתוב בתחלה "ויפלו פניו"....

Ibn Ezra: Lifting of the face, because it is written earlier "and his face fell...."

רמב"ן: אם תטיב יהיה לך יתר שאת על אחיך, כי אתה הבכור....

Ramban: If you will improve, you will have dignity over your brother since you are the firstborn....

מלביי"ם: גילה לו שאין חפץ לה' במנחה רק הנה שמוע מזבח טוב ועקר הוא שתיטיב מעשיך, לא הטבת המשאת והמנח, מה שתיטיב את המשאת לא ירצה בעיניו, כי בין אם תיטיב שאת ובין אם לא תיטיב את המשאת, אין בזה שום מעלה.

Malbim: He revealed to him that God does not want an offering, rather "obeying is more important than a good offering" (I Shmuel 15:22). And the essence is that you should improve your actions, not the improvement of the offering (משאת) and the mincha... for if you improve the offering or if you don't, it has no significance....

Questions:

1. What is the problem in the text that all of the commentators are addressing?

2. What is the meaning of the word שאת according to each commentator?

3. Punctuate the verse according to the Malbim and according to the other three commentators. How does the message of the verse according to the Malbim differ from the message according to the other three?

4. How does the quote from I Shmuel 15:22 support the interpretation of the Malbim?

Suggested Answers:

1. The word שאת has multiple meanings.

2.　　*Radak – forgiveness (as in נשא עון in Shemot 34:7)*
　　　Ibn Ezra – lifting up one's countenance (as in ישא פניו in Bamidbar 6:26)
　　　Ramban – dignity (as in יתר שאת in Bereishit 49:3)
　　　Malbim – offering (as in משאת כפי in Tehilim 141:2)

3.　　*Radak, etc. –*
　　　הלא אם תיטיב, שאת: ואם לא תיטיב, לפתח חטאת רובץ.
　　　Malbim –
　　　הלא אם תיטיב שאת ואם לא תיטיב, לפתח חטאת רובץ.

According to the other three commentators, Cain can protect himself from further sin by correcting his sacrifice. According to the Malbim, correcting the sacrifice will not have an impact. He must correct his general ethic and his actions in order to prevent further sin.

4.　　*The verse refers to an incident in which Shaul brought a sacrifice before Shmuel's arrival even though he had been told to wait for Shmuel. Shmuel informs him that bringing a nice sacrifice is not of value if general obedience to God's will is lacking.*

D. 4:8 –

מדרש רבה: ויאמר קין אל הבל אחיו ויהי בהיותם בשדה - על
מה היו מדיינים? אמרו: בואו ונחלוק את העולם. אחד נטל את
הקרקעות ואחד נטל את המיטלטלין. דין אמר: ארעא דאת
קאם עלה-דידי (זה אמר: הארץ אשר אתה עומד עליה שלי
היא). ודין אמר: מה דאת לבש- דידי (וזה אמר: מה שאתה לובש
שלי הוא). דין אמר: חלוץ! דין אמר: פרח! מתוך כך: "ויקם קין
אל הבל אחיו ויהרגהו".

ר' יהושע דסכנין בשם ר' לוי אמר: שניהם נטלו את
הקרקעות, ושניהם נטלו את המיטלטלין. ועל מה היו מידיינין?
אלא זה אמר: בתחומי בית המקדש ייבנה, וזה אומר: בתחומי
בית המקדש ייבנה... ומתוך כך "ויקם קין אל הבל אחיו
ויהרגהו".

יהודה בר' אמי אמר: על חוה הראשונה היו מידיינין.

Midrash Rabbah: Then Cain said to Hevel while they
were in the field. What were they arguing about? They said:
Come and let us divide up the world. One took the land
and the other took the movable property. The former said:
'The land that you are standing on belongs to me,' and the
latter said: 'The clothes that you are wearing belong to me.'
The latter said: 'Take them off !' and the former said: 'Get
off !' The result: 'Cain rose up against his brother Hevel
and killed him.'

Rabbi Yehoshua of Sakhnin quotes R. Levi: Each took
both land and movable property. What did they argue
about? One said: 'The Temple will be built on my property,' and the other said: 'The Temple will be built on my
property....' As a result, 'Cain rose up against Hevel his
brother and killed him.'

Yehudah the son of R. Ami: They were arguing over
Chava....

רש"י: נכנס עמו בדברי ריב ומצה להתגולל עליו ולהרגו, ויש
בזה מדרשי אגדה אך זה ישובו של מקרא.

Rashi: "He started to argue and fight with him in order to
fall on him and kill him. There is Midrash on this, but the
above is the plain meaning of the verse.

Questions:

1. What is the problem in the text?

2. Why does Rashi refrain from bringing one of the answers
suggested by the Midrash? Why does he consider his interpretation to be the simple meaning?

Suggested Answers:

*1. The text begins to describe a dialogue between Cain and Hevel, but the
dialogue is missing.*

*2. The Midrash presents three plausible explanations as to what was said
in the argument between Cain and Hevel. In these examples, however,
each protagonist has an equal claim. This is not consistent with the text,
which clearly sees Cain as the initiator of the argument. Rashi indicates
that the content of the argument was irrelevant because Cain was just
looking for a pretext to struggle with Hevel.*

E. 4:9 – Textual Comparison

רש"י: אי הבל אחיך?: ליכנס עמו בדברי נחת, אולי ישוב
ויאמר: "אני הרגתיו וחטאתי לך".

Rashi: Where is your brother Hevel?: To enter into pleas-
ant conversation with him so that perhaps he would say: "I
killed and I have sinned to you."

Verse 3:9 – And God called to Adam and he said to him, "Where are you?"

רש"י (ג, ט) : איכה? : יודע היה היכן הוא, אלא ליכנס עמו בדברים, שלא יהא נבהל להשיב אם יענישהו פתאום. וכן בקין אמר לו : אי הבל אחיך?

Rashi (3:9): Where are you?: He knew where he was, but it was to enter into conversation so he wouldn't be too confused to answer if he would punish him suddenly. And similarly in the case of Cain he said: "Where is your brother Hevel?"

Questions:

1. What is the difficulty in the two verses?

2. How does Rashi solve the difficulty similarly in both cases?

3. What is different about the two cases?

Suggested Answers:

1. In both cases, God already knows the information. If so, why does He ask the question?

2. Rashi indicates that in both cases, God was using the question as a way of engaging Adam and Cain in conversation so they could confess their sins.

3. In chapter 3, Adam is hiding and seems to have a sense of embarrassment or remorse for what he did. Cain does not hide and seems to respond in a rather brazen way in which he does not take responsibility for his act.

F. 4:13-14

רש״י: גדול עוני מנשוא, בתמיה, אתה טוען עליונים ותחתונים, ועוני אי אפשר לטעון?

Rashi: My sin is too great to bear: It is a question. You bear the sins of those in the upper and lower worlds, but my sin you cannot bear?

ספורנו: גדול עוני מנשוא. אחר שראה שהא-ל יתברך משגיח בפרטים בהחלט, חשב שידע בלי ספק שאינו שב מחטאו בהיותו מתחרט אלא מפני העונש. והיה כל מוצאי יהרגני. ויהיה העונש גדול מאד ממה שגזרת.

Sforno: My sin is too great to bear: After he saw that God certainly supervises the details, he thought that He knew without a doubt that he didn't repent from his sin out of remorse, but rather because of the punishment. And anyone who finds me will kill me: And it will be a much more severe punishment than you decreed.

רמב״ן: גדול עוני מנשוא: והנכון בפשט שהוא וידוי, אמר אמת כי עוני גדול מלסלוח, וצדיק אתה ה׳ וישר משפטיך, אף על פי שענשת אותי הרבה מאד... אבל מה אעשה כי כל מוצאי יהררגני, ואתה בחסדך הרבים לא חייבת אותי מיתה.

Ramban: My sin is too great to bear: The simple meaning is that it is a confession. He said: "It is true that my sin is too great to forgive, and you God are righteous and just in your judgement, even though you punished me severely....But what will I do, because anyone who finds me will kill me; and you in your kindness did not find me guilty of death.

Questions:

1. Rashi's use of the term בתמיה, turning the verse into a question, is difficult because one could essentially change the entire meaning of the Torah by inserting question marks. What compels Rashi to use בתמיה in this case?

2. How do Sforno and Ramban alternatively understand the phrase ?הן גרשת אותי מעל פני האדמה...

3. What wording in the text suggests to Sforno to interpret the verse as he does?

4. Demonstrate the difference between the three interpretations by punctuating the phrase גדול עוני מנשוא with a period, a question mark, or an exclamation point.

5. Was Cain repentant according to each commentator?

Suggested Answers:

1. In the continuation of the verse, Cain seems to be complaining about the punishment that he received (...הן גרשת אותי). If he is acknowledging the gravity of his sin, such a complaint would be inconsistent.

2. According to both commentators, Cain is claiming that the punishment of expulsion will in reality be more severe than God intended as it will ultimately lead to his death, and God had not sentenced him to death.

3. Sforno gives significance to what is missing in the verse – that Cain never says specifically "I have sinned." Rather, the content of the verse deals with the issue of punishment. He therefore concludes that Cain repents because of the punishment.

4. *Rashi – ?*
    Sforno – .
    Ramban – !

5. *Rashi – Cain never really accepts the severity of his act and does not find the punishment justified.*
    Sforno – Cain did repent, but it was not a complete repentance through recognition of his sin (תשובה מאהבה). Rather, it was based on the punishment (תשובה מיראה).
    Ramban – Cain repented completely and genuinely.

G. 4:15

רש"י: לכן כל הרג קין : זה אחד מן המקראות שקצרו דבריהם ורמזו ולא פירשו : לכן כל הורג קין, לשון גערה... כך וכך עונשו ולא פירש עונשו. שבעתים יקם : איני רוצה להנקם מקין עכשיו, לסוף שבעה דורות אני נוקם נקמתי.

Rashi: Therefore one who kills Cain: This is one of the verses that the Torah shortened and hinted but did not explain. "Therefore one who kills Cain" is the language of scolding....such and such is his punishment, but it did not specify the punishment שבעתיים יוקם: I do not want to take vengeance on Cain now. At the end of seven generations I will take vengeance upon him.

ספורנו: אני אומר לכל מי שהוא מוכן להרוג קין שאני גוזר שתהיה הנקמה על חטאו שבעה פעמים פעמיים.

Sforno: I say to anyone who is prepared to kill Cain that I decree that the punishment for his sin will be 14 fold (seven times doubled).

Questions:

1. To what difficulty in the text are both commentators reacting?

2. What is the difference in their solutions? Demonstrate the difference by translating and punctuating the verse according to each commentator.

3. How do their interpretations relate to their interpretations of verses 13–14?

Suggested Answers:

1. The phrase שבעתים יקם is ambiguous and does not seem to complete the previous clause.

2. According to Rashi, the verse is incomplete. This phrase relates to the timing of the implementation of Cain's punishment, but does not relate to the previous clause at all. The punishment for one who kills Cain prematurely (the completion of the previous clause) is implied but not written.

According to Sforno, the phrase describes the punishment for killing Cain by its severity, thus completing the previous clause. Thus, the grammatical structure of the verse is correct.

Rashi – For anyone who kills Cain _____ [will be punished]; he [Cain] will be avenged [for the murder of Hevel] in seven generations.

Sforno – For anyone who kills Cain will be punished fourteenfold.

3. According to Rashi, Cain did not repent and is still deserving of a punishment. As such, verse 15 indicates that the punishment will be deferred, but not cancelled. Sforno, on the other hand, contends that Cain did repent and, as such, verse 15 indicates that he is not to be punished. Ramban agrees with Sforno's interpretation of this verse.

H. 4:16

רש״י : יצא בהכנעה כגונב דעת העליונה.

Rashi: He went out submissively, as one who deceived God.

Questions:

1. What is the difficulty in the text to which Rashi is reacting?

2. How does Rashi's comment connect to his previous comments on this section?

Suggested Answers:

1. How can one leave God, if God's presence fills the entire universe?

2. Rashi's comment is consistent with his commentary throughout this chapter. He sees Cain as one who never really takes responsibility for his actions, but does what he needs to do in order to save himself.

Educational Message

This unit has several educational messages:

1. The Nature of Conflict – The comparison between the Midrash and Rashi's commentary on verse 8 involves a look at the roots of conflict. The Midrash brings three opinions that base the conflict between Cain and Hevel on issues that are the sources of much of the conflict in the world – possession of property, religion, and sexuality. Rashi posits that sibling rivalry need not be based on a particular issue, as in the case of Cain's enmity toward Hevel.

2. Merit vs. Birthright – Cain's position will ultimately be determined by the quality of his behavior rather than by rights that come to him by virtue of his placement in the family (verses 3–7). The importance of the quality of one's actions as opposed to rote performance is emphasized in the story relating to the offering (verses 3–7) and in the controversy between the commentators regarding the quality of Cain's repentance (verses 13–16).

3. Responsibility for One's Actions and the Possibility of Repentance – Cain's inability to take responsibility for his actions is emphasized in verses 3–7 and in verse 9. According to Rashi, this character trait remains with Cain throughout the chapter. According to Sforno and Ramban, a change takes place in verse 13. In their opinions, once Cain takes responsibility for his actions, he is able to engage in repentance. The concept of repentance is introduced in verses 6–7. The controversy between Sforno and Ramban on verses 13–14 raise the distinction between repentance based on fear (תשובה מיראה) and sincere repentance (תשובה מאהבה).

SOURCES

Much of the material in this book is taken from courses that Nechama Leibowitz delivered in 1990–1992 under the auspices of the Jerusalem Fellows Program, including courses on "Teaching Methodology," "Rashi and Ramban," "Ibn Ezra," and "The Book of Yirmiyahu." Many of Nechama's methodological principles and examples from the text of the Tanach are found in her writings as well, frequently in more than one source. The following list is designed to provide the reader with as many accessible sources as possible for the concepts and textual examples found in this book. When the information is found in more than one source, the most accessible source is provided.

Chapter 1–2

The principles put forth in these chapters were gleaned from a course on teaching methodology given by Nechama in 1990–91. Some of these ideas are discussed, as well, in a letter that Nechama wrote to Rafi Aaronson that was published in פרקי נחמה, Eliner Library, Jerusalem 2001, pp. 653–656. An English translation of this letter appears in *Jewish Educational Leadership*, Spring 2003 (1:1), pp. 52–53. Nechama's introductory method of dividing the chapter is demonstrated a number of times in הוראת פרשני התורה: שמות, Eliner Library, Jerusalem 2003. The division of Chapter 1 of Shemot is found on pages 14–17 of that work. Other examples presented in chapters 1 and 2 of this book are provided by the author.

Chapter 3

Many of the concepts discussed in this chapter are found in Nechama's article entitled "Rashi's Criteria for Citing *Midrashim*" which appears in *Torah Insights*, Eliner Library, Jerusalem, 1995. The examples utilized are taken from the following sources:

1) Cain and Hevel (Bereishit 4:8) – *Rashi's Commentary on the Torah*, Open University of Israel, Tel Aviv, 1990, pp. 367–368
2) Eldad and Medad (Bamidbar 11:26–28) – *Rashi's Commentary on the Torah*, Open University of Israel, Tel Aviv, 1990, p. 464

Chapter 4

The questions in sections A, B, D, E, F, and H of this chapter are taken from Nechama's *gilayon* for Vayera 5721. The suggested answers are provided by Yitshak Reiner from his publication of the gilyanot in *Darchei Noam: Bereshit I*, Jewish National Fund, Jerusalem, 1999, pp. 31–40. The question and answer in section E were modified somewhat by the author, and in section F an additional question and answer were added by the author. The question in section C is taken from Nechama's *gilayon* for Vayera 5716, and the suggested answer is provided by the author. The question and answer in section G are provided by the author based on Nechama's discussion of this section in:

Hora'at Parshanei HaTorah: Bereishit, Eliner Library, Jerusalem, 2003, pp. 68–69.

Chapter 5

The principles discussed in this chapter were gleaned from Nechama's courses. Many of the ideas are also found in chapter 6 of *Rashi's Commentary on the Torah*, Open University of Israel, Tel Aviv, 1990. The examples utilized are from the following sources:

1) The Covenants with Avimelech (Bereishit 21:22–34; 26:14–33) – provided by the author.
2) Moshe Leaves the Palace (Shemot 2:11–17) – *Studies in Shemot*, The World Zionist Organization, Jerusalem, 1976, p. 40
3) Honor and Fear of Parents (Shemot 20:12; Vayikra 19:3) – *Rashi's Commentary on the Torah*, Open University of Israel, Tel Aviv, 1990, p. 222
4) Shabbat (Shemot 20:11; Devarim 5:16) – *Gilayon* Yitro 5718 published in *Darchei Noam: Shemot I*, Jewish National Fund, Jerusalem, 1999, pp. 39–40
5) Pharoah's Dream (Bereishit 41:3; 41:19–21) – *Gilayon* Miketz 5715
6) Eliezer's Mission (Bereishit 24:3–4, 7, 22; 24:37, 40, 47) – *Rashi's Commentary on the Torah*, Open University of Israel, Tel Aviv, 1990, p. 258
7) Moshe vs. Pharoah (Shemot 3:16, 18; 4:29–30; 5:1) – *Studies in Shemot*, The World Zionist Organization, Jerusalem, 1976, p. 91–92

Chapter 6

Most of the information and examples in this chapter are taken from *Rashi's Commentary on the Torah*, Open University of Israel, Tel Aviv, 1990. The examples utilized are taken from the following sources:

1) Repetition of Words
a) Akeidat Yitzchak (Bereishit 22:7–8) – *Rashi's Commentary on the Torah*, Open University of Israel, Tel Aviv, 1990, p. 79
b) Be Fruitful and Multiply (Bereishit 9:1, 7) – *Rashi's Commentary on the Torah*, Open University of Israel, Tel Aviv, 1990, p. 75

2) Similar Words
a) Be Fruitful and Multiply (Bereishit 1:22) – *Rashi's Commentary on the Torah*, Open University of Israel, Tel Aviv, 1990, p. 80
b) Yaacov's Fear (Bereishit 32:8) – *Rashi's Commentary on the Torah*, Open University of Israel, Tel Aviv, 1990, p. 81

3) The Positive and the Negation of Its Opposite
a) Yosef's Pit (Bereishit 37:24) – *Rashi's Commentary on the Torah*, Open University of Israel, Tel Aviv, 1990, p. 83
b) The Midwives (Shemot 1:17) – Ibn Ezra , *Rashi's Commentary on the Torah*, Open University of Israel, Tel Aviv, 1990, p. 89

4) Deviation in Word Order
a) Lavan and Betuel (Bereishit 24:50) – *Rashi's Commentary on the Torah*, Open University of Israel, Tel Aviv, 1990, p. 213
b) Rachel and Leah (Bereishit 31:4) – *Rashi's Commentary on the Torah*, Open University of Israel, Tel Aviv, 1990, p. 213
c) Yaacov's Ladder (Bereishit 28:12) – *Rashi's Commentary on the Torah*, Open University of Israel, Tel Aviv, 1990, p. 216
d) The Manna (Shemot 16:20) – *Rashi's Commentary on the Torah*, Open University of Israel, Tel Aviv, 1990, p. 219
e) The Daughter's of Tzlafchad (Bamidbar 27:2) – *Rashi's Commentary on the Torah*, Open University of Israel, Tel Aviv, 1990, p. 213
f) Noach and his Family (Bereishit 6:18, 7:7, 8:16, 18) – *Rashi's Commentary on the Torah*, Open University of Israel, Tel Aviv, 1990, pp. 222–223

g) Moshe and the Tribes of Gad and Reuven (Bamidbar 32: 16, 24-26) – Studies in Bamidbar, Eliner Library, Jerusalem, 1993, Mattot Iyun #2

h) Yosef Distibutes Provisions (Bereishit 41:57) – *Rashi's Commentary on the Torah*, Open University of Israel, Tel Aviv, 1990, p. 232

i) Yosef and the Wife of Potiphar (Bereishit 39:17) – *Rashi's Commentary on the Torah*, Open University of Israel, Tel Aviv, 1990, p. 232

j) Yaacov and Lavan (Bereishit 30:29–30) – *Rashi's Commentary on the Torah*, Open University of Israel, Tel Aviv, 1990, p. 227–228

k) Pharoah and Moshe (Shemot 12:32) – *Rashi's Commentary on the Torah*, Open University of Israel, Tel Aviv, 1990, p. 228

5) Deviations in Chronological Order

a) Adam and Chava (Berishit 4:1) – *Rashi's Commentary on the Torah*, Open University of Israel, Tel Aviv, 1990, p. 128

b) Moshe Ascends the Mountain (Shemot 24:1, 12) – *Rashi's Commentary on the Torah*, Open University of Israel, Tel Aviv, 1990, p. 129

c) Sarah Becomes Pregnant (Bereishit 21:1) – *Rashi's Commentary on the Torah*, Open University of Israel, Tel Aviv, 1990, p. 131

d) Pesach Sheni (Bamidbar 1:1–2, 9:1) – from Nechama's course

e) The Mishkan and the Golden Calf (Shemot 31:18) – from Nechama's course

f) Yitro and the Giving of the Torah (Shemot 18:1) – from Nechama's course

g) Korach (Bamidbar 16:1-3) – from Nechama's course

6) Internal Inconsistency

a) The Burning Bush (Shemot 3:5) - *Rashi's Commentary on the Torah*, Open University of Israel, Tel Aviv, 1990, p. 146

b) They Camped at Mt. Sinai (Shemot 19:12) – Example provided by author

c) The Garden of Eden (Bereishit 3:11, 13–15) – *Rashi's Commentary on the Torah*, Open University of Israel, Tel Aviv, 1990, p. 260

d) The Six Days of Creation (Bereishit 1:5, 8, 13, 19, 22, 31) – *Rashi's Commentary on the Torah*, Open University of Israel, Tel Aviv, 1990, p. 263

e) The Creation of Man (Bereishit 1:27, 2:7–8) – *Rashi's Commentary on the Torah*, Open University of Israel, Tel Aviv, 1990, pp. 268–269

f) The Manna (Bamidbar 11:4–6, 7–8) – *Rashi's Commentary on the Torah*, Open University of Israel, Tel Aviv, 1990, p. 267

Chapter 7

1) The Key Word

a) The Bikkurim Declaration (Devarim 26:1–11) – *Gilayon* Ki Tavo 5719

b) Pharoah and Yosef (Bereishit 41:25, 28, 32); The Cries of Bnai Yisroel in Egypt (Shemot 2:23–25); Moshe's Response to the Tribes of Reuven and Gad (Bamidbar 32:20–23) – *Gilayon* Miketz 5711

2) What's in a Name?

a) Yishmael (Bereishit 21) – *Gilayon* Vayera 5713

b) Yosef (Bereishit 37: 18–32) – from Nechama's course

c) The Golden Calf (Shemot 32:1–14) – *Gilayon* Ki Tissa 5722

3) Biblical Dialogue – The principles and all of the examples from this chapter are found in an article by Nechama entitled ויאמר...ויאמר which appears in *Pirke Nechama*, Eliner Library, Jerusalem 2001, pp. 495–502. Nechama also addressed this issue in her *Gilayon* Lech Lecha 5717.

4) Association

a) Causality (Vayikra 25) – *Rashi's Commentary on the Torah*, Open University of Israel, Tel Aviv, 1990, pp. 425–426

b) Limitation:

    1) Agricultural Laws (Devarim 22:9-12) – *Rashi's Commentary on the Torah*, Open University of Israel, Tel Aviv, 1990, p. 423

    2) War (Devarim 19:16–21, 20:1–9) – *Rashi's Commentary on the Torah*, Open University of Israel, Tel Aviv, 1990, p. 424

5) Parallelism – This concept is discussed in *Rashi's Commentary on the Torah*, Open University of Israel, Tel Aviv, 1990, pp. 91–93. The examples utilized are taken from the following sources:

a) Shimon and Levi (Bereishit 49:5–7) – *Gilayon* Vayechi 5714

b) Anger and Wrath (Tehillim 78:38) – from Nechama's courses

Chapter 8

Although some of the sources and questions in this chapter are found as well in Nechama's *gilyonot*, most of the questions were formulated by the author based on a selection of the sources and the analysis in Nechama's iyunim on Vayikra (Hebrew Edition). The examples utilized are taken from the following sources:

1) Verse19:2 – *New Studies in Vayikra*, Eliner Library, Jerusalem, 1993, Kedoshim Iyun # 2

2) Verse19:3 – *New Studies in Vayikra*, Eliner Library, Jerusalem, 1993, Kedoshim Iyun # 3

3) Verses 19:9-12 – *New Studies in Vayikra*, Eliner Library, Jerusalem, 1993, Kedoshim Iyun # 4

4) Verse 19:13 – *New Studies in Vayikra*, Eliner Library, Jerusalem, 1993, Kedoshim Iyun # 5

5) Verse 19:14 – *New Studies in Vayikra*, Eliner Library, Jerusalem, 1993, Kedoshim Iyunim # 6–7

6) Verse 19:17 – *New Studies in Vayikra*, Eliner Library, Jerusalem, 1993, Kedoshim Iyun # 11

7) Verse 19:18 – *New Studies in Vayikra*, Eliner Library, Jerusalem, 1993, Kedoshim Iyunim # 12–13

Chapter 9

1) Verse 4:1 – *Rashi's Commentary on the Torah*, Open University of Israel, Tel Aviv, 1990, p. 128

2) Verses 4:3–4 - *Rashi's Commentary on the Torah*, Open University of Israel, Tel Aviv, 1990, p. 261

3) Verses 4:6–7 – The analysis of Rashi and Malbim is found in *Gilayon* Bereishit 5716; Nechama discussed the other commentators as well in her course.

4) Verse 4:8 – *Rashi's Commentary on the Torah*, Open University of Israel, Tel Aviv, 1990, p. 367–368

5) Verse 4:9 – *Gilayon* Bereishit 5702

6) Verses 13–14 – The analysis of Rashi and Ramban is found in *Limud Parshanei HaTorah U'drachim Lehora'atam: Sefer Bereishit*, World Zionist Organization, Jerusalem, 1975, pp. 10–11; the commentary of Sforno was added by the author.

7) Verse 4:15 – The analysis of Rashi is found in *Limud Parshanei HaTorah U'drachim Lehora'atam: Sefer Bereishit*, World Zionist Organization, Jerusalem, 1975, p. 11–12; the commentary of Sforno was added by the author.

8) Verse 4:16 – *Limud Parshanei HaTorah U'drachim Lehora'atam: Sefer Bereishit*, World Zionist Organization, Jerusalem, 1975, p. 13

APPENDICES

COMMON TEXTUAL DIFFICULTIES

NECHAMA REMEMBERED: דברי זכרון

BIBLIOGRAPHY –
NECHAMA LEIBOWITZ'S PUBLISHED WORKS

COMMON TEXTUAL DIFFICULTIES

I. The Word
    A.   Uncommon Words

            Ex. Shemot 16:31 כצפיחת

    B.   Words with Specialized Usages

            Ex. Utensils of the Mishkan, Vestments of the Priests (i.e., חשן, ציץ)

    C.   Words with Multiple Meanings

            Ex. כל בשר = all people or all living things – see Bereishit 6:19, 6:17, 6:19, 6:21; Vayikra 13:24; Yeshayahu 66:23

    D.   A Word Used Outside of Its Usual Meaning

            Ex. Shemot 23:5 עזב תעזב

II. Extraneous Language (לשון יתרה)
    A.   Repetition of Words

            Ex. Bereishit 22:11 אברהם אברהם

    B.   Repetition of Synonyms

            Ex. Bereishit 1:22 פרו ורבו

    C.   Positive and Negative Restatement

            Ex. Bereishit 40:33 ולא זכר... וישכחהו

    D.   Extraneous Modifiers

            Ex. Bereishit 28:5 רבקה אם יעקב ועשו

    E.   Extraneous Pronouns

            Ex. Bereishit 9:7 **ואתם** פרו ורבו

III. Lacunas (לשון חסרה)
A. Missing Subjects

   Ex. Bereishit 48:1 ויאמר ליוסף
B. Missing Objects

   Ex. Bereishit 12:8 ויעתק משם ההרה
C. Incomplete Sentences (מקרא קצר, משפט גזום)

   Ex. Shemot 22:22 אם ענה תענה אותו

IV. Grammatical and Syntactical Problems
A. Homonyms
   1. Different Tenses

      Ex. Bereishit 29:6,9 באה
   2. Different Conjugations

      Ex. Bamidbar 22:25 ותלחץ
   3. Different Roots

      Ex. Yeshayahu 21:13, Tehillim 137:2 תלינו
B. Indefinite Subjects

   Ex. Bereishit 44:22 ויעזב את אביו ומת
C. Indefinite Modifiers

   Ex. Bereishit 25:28 כי ציד בפיו
D. Inconsistency Between Parts of a Sentence

   Ex. 1 – Gender: Noun – Adjective Shemot 3:5
   אדמת קדש הוא

   Ex. 2 – Number: Subject – Verb Shemot 19:2
   ויחנו במדבר ויחן ישראל

The categories and examples in this list are taken from *Peirush Rashi laTorah: Iyunim beShitato (Rashi's Commentary on the Torah)*, by Nechama Leibowitz and Moshe Arend, Tel Aviv, The Open University of Israel, 1990.

NECHAMA REMEMBERED
דברי זכרון

A MEMORIAL TRIBUTE TO NECHAMA LEIBOWITZ זצ״ל

On the 5th of Nissan, we commemorate the yahrzeit of our revered teacher, Nechama Leibowitz זצ״ל.

The Master Teacher

Nechama requested that on her grave stone she be identified simply as "*morah*," a teacher. It is a characteristically simple epitaph, but in Nechama's case it speaks volumes. Certainly, Nechama stands out as one of the master teachers of Torah in our generation, both in terms of her academic writings and her insights on pedagogy. But, perhaps, the most important quality that identified Nechama as a teacher was the relationship that she established with her students. One could not sit anonymously in Nechama's shiurim. She demanded that each student write the answers to her questions. She checked them all on the spot and gave responses. Thus, she got to know her students. Similarly, her *gilyonot* were distributed far and wide. Literally thousands of students would send their answers in to Nechama by mail. She would examine them all personally and respond. Nechama was a favorite of the Israeli Postal Service.

Respect for the Common Person

Even by mail, Nechama got to know her students. It happened once that she received answers to the *gilyonot* on a weekly basis from an unidentified respondent. Curious as to who this dedicated student might be, Nechama eventually asked that she identify herself. It turned out that the correspondent was a waitress from Ashkelon. Nechama could count among her students some of the accomplished rabbis and educators of our generation. She rarely spoke about them, but she loved to mention the waitress from Ashkelon. She was truly gratified and inspired by the dedication of the common people to Torah study and Judaism.

Only in Israel

Nechama similarly took pride in the Torah knowledge and religious sentiment of the "man on the street" in Israel. These qualities often manifested themselves in encounters on Israeli buses and taxis. Nechama loved to recount these stories. The following are two of her favorites:

1. An older gentleman boarded a rather full bus, and a young boy stood up to offer his seat. The man said to the boy: "Because of which part of the verse did you stand up for me?" (The man was referring to the verse in Vayikra 19:32 which states that one should rise before the elderly and honor the aged. The commentators indicate that one reference is to the elderly and one is to the wise.) The boy responded: "Both." And then the man took the seat. Nechama always ended the story with a smile, stating: "And nobody had to say which verse they were referring to!"

2. Nechama once entered a taxi at a hotel on a Friday. The concierge came out and told the driver that he had a guest who wanted to travel the next day (Shabbat) to Haifa for a very good fare. The driver declined, and the concierge tried to entice him by increasing

the fare. The driver was clearly not wealthy, but he continued to refuse until he finally got angry with the concierge and left. For the entire ride, the cab driver kept muttering under his breath : " I don't travel on Shabbat. I don't travel on Shabbat. I don't travel on Shabbat ! On Shabbat I go to the Beit Knesset to be with God !" In telling the story, Nechama would repeat the last line several times. She was struck by the purity of this simple man's religious sentiment.

Love of the Land, the People, and the State

Nechama settled in Israel before the establishment of the state. Her bus stories also included tales of bus rides from Tel Aviv to Jerusalem under armed attack before the state was established. She took great pride in the accomplishments of the Jewish people in the State of Israel. Once again, it was the special sense of caring that most impressed Nechama. Following Operation Shlomo in which 14,000 Ethiopians were brought to Israel in one weekend, Nechama could not stop marveling at the fact that "each of them had a place to sleep." Nechama was troubled when she observed a lack of such caring. She entered the hospital for the first time in her life when she was 87 years old. When visiting her in the hospital, she expressed her dismay that the doctors could talk to each other about the patients as if the patients were not there. This was antithetical to Nechama the teacher. This certainly shouldn't happen in a Jewish hospital.

Nechama's love of Eretz Yisrael and Medinat Yisrael was so strong that she could not be persuaded to leave the country. Many times, her students wanted her to come to Chutz La'aretz to train teachers. She never agreed to leave Israel, even for such an important purpose.

"The Honor of the King's Daughter is Within"

Nechama's ability to respect and value others was a reflection of her deep humility. Many in her position would have developed a sense of self importance. Nechama truly did not recognize her own greatness. I once received a call from Yitzchak Reiner from Nechama's apartment. Nechama got on the phone and said: "Shmuel, do you remember me?" She was not being sarcastic. Nechama lived in a very modest two room apartment. Her walls were lined with the *gilyonot* that she had produced over the years. She could not be convinced to take a gift. Her students often tried unsuccessfully to devise a method of giving her a gift as a token of appreciation. The only thing that I ever saw her accept were candies that she could place on her table to pass around to the students during shiurim. Nechama did not make her Torah study a vehicle for self aggrandizement on either the financial or the psychological level. She embodied the mishna from Pirke Avot: "If you have learned much Torah do not ascribe greatness to yourself, because for that purpose you were created." (Avot 2:9)

An Honest Encounter with the Text

It was perhaps Nechama's humility as well that enabled her to be the outstanding Torah scholar that she was. She came to learn Torah from the great medieval commentators. She came to hear them speak, not to have them speak for her. It was this sense of honest scholarship that she imparted to her students. It was this sense of humility that endeared her to them.

Her grave stone reads simply "*morah*." That is her legacy. The fact that her *gilyonot* are still utilized, that her Torah is still learned, is the greatest and most meaningful memorial that could be established for Nechama, our *morah*.

Nechama did not leave any children to say kaddish for her. She did, however, leave a host of students to remember her and pray for the ascent of her soul. May her soul be bound up in the bond of life.

BIBLIOGRAPHY

Nechama Leibowitz's Published Works

The following is a list of the works of Nechama Leibowitz that have been published in book form. A full bibliography including a listing of articles and collections of articles by Nechama can be found in:

Pirke Nechama, edited by Moshe Arend, Gavriel Cohen, and Rut Ben-Meir (Eliner Press, World Zionist Organization, 2001).

A very important component of Nechama's publications, the *gilyonot*, do not appear in book form. These study guides on parshat hashavua were published weekly by Nechama from 1942 until 1972. Many of the *gilyonot* were accompanied by teachers' guides ("*alonei hadracha*"). These works are available in a number of university libraries in Israel and in some Judaica libraries.

עברית

עיונים בספר בראשית, ספריית אלינר, ההסתדרות הציונית העולמית, תשכ״ו.

עיונים חדשים בספר שמות, ספריית אלינר, ההסתדרות הציונית העולמית, תש״ל.

עיונים חדשים בספר ויקרא, ספריית אלינר, ההסתדרות הציונית העולמית, תשמ״ג.

עיונים בספר במדבר, ספריית אלינר, ההסתדרות הציונית העולמית, תשנ"ו.

עיונים בספר דברים, ספריית אלינר, ההסתדרות הציונית העולמית, תשנ"ד.

ללמוד וללמד תנ"ך, ספריית אלינר, ההסתדרות הציונית העולמית, תשנ"ה.

פירוש רש"י לתורה: עיונים בשיטתו (עם משה ארנד), 2 כרכים, האוניברסיטה הפתוחה, תש"ן.

לימוד פרשני התורה ודרכים להוראתם: ספר בראשית, המחלקה לחינוך ולתרבות תורניים בגולה, ההסתדרות הציונית העולמית, תשל"ה (מהדורה חדשה ע"י ספריית אלינר, תשס"ג).

הוראת פרשני התורה: שמות, ספריית אלינר, ההסתדרות הציונית העולמית, תשס"ג.

גליונות לעיון בספר ירמיהו, המחלקה לחינוך ולתרבות תורניים בגולה, ההסתדרות הציונית העולמית, תשל"ד.

פרקי נחמה וגאולה (עם מאיר וייס), ספריית אלינר, ההסתדרות הציונית העולמית.

English

Studies in Bereshit, Eliner Press, World Zionist Organization, 1976.

Studies in Shemot, Eliner Press, World Zionist Organization, 1976.

Studies in Vayikra, Eliner Press, World Zionist Organization, 1993.

Studies in Bamidbar, Eliner Press, World Zionist Organization, 1993.

Studies in Devarim, Eliner Press, World Zionist Organization, 1993.

Torah Insights, Eliner Press, World Zionist Organization, 1995.

Leaders Guide to the Book of Psalms, Hadassah, WZOA, 1971.

(Note: *Studies in Parshat Hashavua* have also been published in French, Spanish , and Dutch.)

Although Nechama's *gilyonot* have not been published in book form, a selection of *gilyonot* and alonei hadracha have been published in print and on the internet, with suggested answers provided by Yitzchak Reiner:

עברית

גליונות לעיון בפרשת השבוע תשנ״ט (עם תשובות ע״י יצחק ריינר), אתר האינטרנט של קק״ל (www.kkl.org.il).

גליונות לעיון בפרשת השבוע תש״ס – תשס״א (עם תשובות ע״י יצחק ריינר), אתר האינטרנט של המועצה העולמית לחינוך תורני www.torahcc.org

דרכי נועם : גליונות לעיון בפרשת השבוע (עם תשובות ע״י יצחק ריינר), בראשית – שמות ב-4 כרכים, קרן קיימת לישראל, תשנ״ט.

English

Darchei Noam: Gilyonot on the Weekly Torah Portion (with answers by Yitshak Reiner), 4 volumes, Jewish National Fund, 1999–2000.
(Note: these booklets have also been published in French, Spanish, Portuguese, and German.)

Gilyonot on the Weekly Torah Portion 5759 (with answers by Yitshak Reiner), Internet Site of the Jewish National Fund (www.kkl.org.il)

Gilyonot on the Weekly Torah Portion 5760-61 (with answers by Yitshak Reiner), Internet Site of the World Council for Torah Education (www.torahcc.org)

In addition to the above resources, a number of questions from Nechama's *gilyonot* relating to the Haggadah of Pesach are found in the following two publications:

Studies on the Haggadah From the Teachings of Nechama Leibowitz, edited by Yitshak Reiner and Shmuel Peerless, Urim Publications, Jerusalem, 2002.

הגדת נחמה: עיונים בהגדה של פסח על-פי הגליונות והשיעורים של נחמה ליבוביץ, בעריכת יצחק ריינר ושמואל פירלס, אורים הוצאה לאור, ירושלים, 2003.

About the Author

Rabbi Shmuel Peerless is the Director of the Center for Jewish School Leadership at Bar-Ilan University's Lookstein Center for Jewish Education in the Diaspora. Previously, he served as the educational director of the Hillel Academy of Dayton, Ohio and the Hebrew Academy of Montreal, and was the director of the World Council for Torah Education. He studied with Nechama Leibowitz for several years and co-authored *Studies on the Haggadah from the Teachings of Nechama Leibowitz* (Urim) and an expanded edition in Hebrew entitled:

הגדת נחמה : עיונים בהגדה של פסח על-פי הגליונות והשיעורים של נחמה ליבוביץ (אורים).